Reading Comprehension Skills and Strategies
Level 5

SADDLEBACK
PUBLISHING · INC.

Saddleback Publishing, Inc.
Three Watson
Irvine, CA 92618-2767
E-Mail: info@sdlback.com
Web site: www.sdlback.com

Development and Production:
The EDGe

ISBN 1-56254-032-7

Printed in the United States of America
06 05 04 03 02 9 8 7 6 5 4 3 2 1

Table of Contents
Skills

About this Series

This unique series is specially created for you by Saddleback Publishing, Inc., as an exciting supplement to reinforce and extend your classroom reading curriculum. *Reading Comprehension Skills and Strategies* can easily be integrated into basic reading curricula as additional reading lessons: as stand-alone strategy and skill instructional lessons; as across-the-curriculum lessons; or as activities for students with special projects, interests, or abilities.

This series is based on the most current research and thought concerning the teaching of reading comprehension. This series not only sharpens traditional reading comprehension skills (main idea, story plot, topic sentence, sequencing, etc.), but it also reinforces the critical reading comprehension strategies that encourage your students to use prior knowledge, experiences, careful thought, and evaluation to help them decide how to practically apply what they know to all reading situations.

Traditional comprehension skills recently have been woven into the larger context of strategy instruction. Today, literacy instruction emphasizes learning strategies—those approaches that coordinate the various reading and writing skills and prior knowledge to make sense to the learner. Our goal in this series is to provide you and your students with the most up-to-date reading comprehension support, while teaching basic skills that can be tested and evaluated.

Reading Comprehension Strategies

- vocabulary knowledge
- activating prior knowledge
- pre-reading—previewing and predicting
- previewing and predicting text
- mental imaging
- self-questioning
- summarizing
- semantic mapping

Saddleback Publishing, Inc., promotes the development of the whole child with particular emphasis on combining solid skill instruction with creativity and imagination. This series gives your students a variety of opportunities to apply reading comprehension strategies as they read, while reinforcing basic reading comprehension skills. In addition, we designed this series to help you make an easy transition between levels (grades 4, 5, and 6) in order to reinforce or enhance needed skill development for individual students.

About this Book

Reading Comprehension Skills and Strategies is designed to reinforce and extend the reading skills of your students. The fun, high-interest fiction and non-fiction selections will spark the interest of even your most reluctant reader. The book offers your students a variety of reading opportunities—reading for pleasure, reading to gather information, and reading to perform a task. A character on each page prompts the student to apply one of the strategies to the reading selection and includes a relevant comprehension skill activity.

Choosing Instructional Approaches

You can use the pages in this book for independent reinforcement or extension, whole group lessons, pairs, or small cooperative groups rotating through an established reading learning center. You may choose to place the activities in a center and reproduce the answer key for self-checking. To ensure the utmost flexibility, the process for managing this is left entirely up to you because you know what works best in your classroom.

Assessment

Assessment and evaluation of student understanding and ability is an ongoing process. A variety of methods and strategies should be used to ensure that the student is being assessed and evaluated in a fair and comprehensive manner. Always keep in mind that the assessment should take into consideration the opportunities the student had to learn the information and practice the skills presented. The strategies for assessment are left for you to determine and are dependent on your students and your particular instructional plan. You will find a Scope & Sequence chart at the back of this book to assist you as you develop your assessment plan.

Learning the meaning of some prefixes and adding them to root words adds lots of new words to your vocabulary. Now, that's cool!

Directions: *Add a prefix to each root word to make a new word. Then write a sentence using each new word.*

Prefixes

un = not	dis = opposite	mid = middle	re = again
trans = across	in = into	mis = bad	sub = under

1. port/ _____

   _____

2. like/ _____

   _____

3. side/ _____

   _____

4. night/ _____

   _____

5. take/ _____

   _____

6. way/ _____

   _____

7. comfortable/ _____

   _____

8. appear/ _____

   _____

9. behave/ _____

   _____

10. honest/ _____

    _____

Name: _____ **Date:** _____

WORD LIST

pedicure   pedal   pedometer   impediment

pedestal   pedestrian   centipede

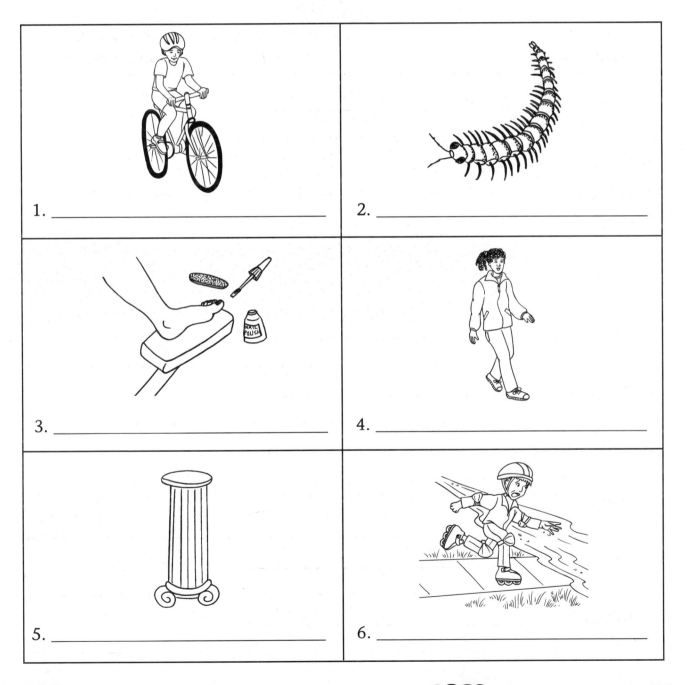

1. _____

2. _____

3. _____

4. _____

5. _____

6. _____

Name: _____   Date: _____

Directions: Add a prefix or a suffix to the root words below to make new words. Write as many new words as you can on the lines below.

PREFIXES AND SUFFIXES

dia — between, across

mega — large

mono — single

epi — over, upon or about

tele — far off, at a distance

micro — small

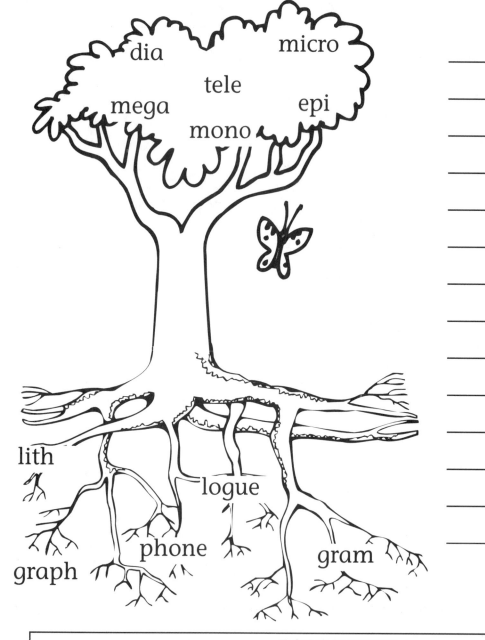

dia micro tele mega epi mono

lith logue phone gram graph

_____

_____

_____

_____

_____

_____

_____

_____

_____

_____

_____

ROOT WORDS

lith — stone

gram — write, draw

logue — word, speech

phone — sound, voice

graph — write

Name: _____   Date: _____

less	able	ive	ful	ness	dis	ing	ly	un
ion	ty	est	under	able	ship	al	fulness	over

1. The king's men have never been _____ loyal. Their loyal _____ is not in question.

2. The Mayberry Marlins might be _____ beat _____ this year. With a record of four wins and no losses they are the only _____ beaten team in the league.

3. The puppy was very skinny and _____ nourished because she was not fed properly by her owners.

4. It was very thought_____ of you to send a get-well card while I was in the hospital. Your thought_____ is appreciated.

5. It's not healthy to be so obsess_____ about how your hair looks. That silly haircut could become an obsess_____.

6. Maggie paid $50 for her concert ticket. I bought mine for $30—Maggie definitely _____ paid!

7. I have been wonder_____ how you like your new school. I think it's wonder_____ that you earned four A's on your first report card.

8. When your parents love you without condition, their love is called _____ condition _____.

9. Derek and Wally are always friend_____ to everyone, but they especially value their unique friend_____ with each other.

10. Our dog is an ador_____ new parent. She just gave birth to six ador_____ puppies.

11. The cat proud____ showed us her new kittens. She is the proud_____ parent on the block.

12. Your suggestions are never use____. I am happy to say all of your ideas are use_____.

13. My greatest happy_____ is mountain-climbing, the higher the better. I am happy_____ when I am standing on top of the mountain.

A prefix changes the meaning of a root word.

Prefix	Meaning	Example
under	lower, not enough, covered by	undercoat
mis	wrong, do badly	miscount
dis	not	disobey

_____ 1. I'm sorry dinner will be late tonight because the oven is broken and the roast is underdone.

   a. overcooked   b. not cooked enough

_____ 2. The market on the corner went out of business because it was mismanaged.

   a. not well supervised   b. well supervised

_____ 3. The employees felt they were being underpaid when they had to work more than eight hours in one day.

   a. not paid enough   b. paid too much

_____ 4. The spacecraft missed the moon by 100 miles because the computer miscalculated.

   a. computed incorrectly   b. broke down

_____ 5. I dislike walking home from school in the rain because my feet always get wet.

   a. enjoy   b. don't enjoy

_____ 6. The people behind us at the theater were talking in an undertone all through the movie.

   a. loud voice   b. whisper

_____ 7. Harold's mother was dissatisfied with her son when he got all C's on his report card.

   a. not happy   b. happy

_____ 8. My mother has put me on a special diet because I am underweight for my height.

   a. weighs too much   b. doesn't weigh enough

_____ 9. Sarah is afraid her sister has misplaced her library book and it is due today.

   a. put in a wrong place   b. forgot

_____ 10. Bryan felt discomfort for a week after he had an accident on his bicycle.

   a. just fine   b. soreness

Name: _____   **Date:** _____

fore = before, in front of	*im* = not	*dis* = reversal

a. im<u>mod</u>est

b. forethought

c. imperfect

d. forecast

e. immature

f. disinfect

g. foresight

h. disrespect

i. immortal

j. foreman

k. impossible

l. disintegrate

m. foremost

n. immovable

o. disqualify

p. impassive

q. foretold

r. dishonest

s. forerunner

t. forefather

u. immeasurable

v. immoderate

1. _____ to plan in advance

2. _____ cannot be moved or changed

3. _____ separate into fragments

4. _____ predict

5. _____ indecent, impudent

6. _a_ rude or impolite

7. _____ not mortal, living forever

8. _____ an ancestor

9. _____ first in importance

10. _____ can't be done

11. _____ not allow to participate

12. _____ not completely grown or developed

13. _____ destroy harmful bacteria

14. _____ not showing any feeling or emotion

15. _____ see or know beforehand

16. _____ without restraint, excessive

17. _____ lying or cheating

18. _____ man in charge

19. _____ cannot be measured, immense

20. _____ having a defect or error

21. _____ previously said

22. _____ person sent ahead to announce something is coming

A suffix is like a caboose — it's always located at the end.

Directions: *Using -er and –est, decide which suffix belongs in the blank of each sentence. You may need to change the spelling of the root word.*

Use the suffix:	When you are comparing:
er	2 things
est	3 or more things

1. Kelly was voted the neat_____ camp scout because she kept her belongings organized alphabetically.

2. They say the bigger you are, the hard_____ you fall. That means if you are the biggest, you fall the hard_____.

3. There is nothing tough_____ than a diamond—it is the tough_____ stone known to humans.

4. Hank is the fast_____ runner on the team, much fast_____ than I am!

5. Coach said those who try the hard_____ will make the team, so I'd better try hard_____.

6. Is traveling by train slow_____ than traveling by bus? What is the slow_____ form of transportation?

7. He is the brav_____ stunt man of all. He is even brav_____ than his father.

8. Brooke cried because she received the small_____ slice of pie. Justin cried because he thought his piece was even small _____.

9. Which is old_____, the Empire State Building or the Eiffel Tower?

10. The Quinn family has ten children; Kelly is young____ than Kyle. Kerry is the young_____.

11. This highway is much busy_____ than it was last year. Soon it will be the busy_____ highway in the state.

12. I have several packages to mail. The light_____ package will cost less to mail. Of the two packages left to mail, this one is light_____.

Name: _____   **Date:** _____

1. As the exam date approached, Jenny became increasingly worried that she was not properly prepared.

2. Many engines are powered by internal combustion.

3. The locomotive came barreling down the track.

4. Even in his maturity, Herbert still loved to collect toy planes.

5. I think the mighty Mississippi is the longest river in the United States.

6. There were too many sailors living in trailers, which made them very combative.

7. Two thoughtful internists assisted the doctor during the operation.

8. I originate from New York, but I don't consider myself a New Yorker.

9. If you followed the directive, there shouldn't be any confusion.

10. Suspicions and assumptions can get you into troubling situations!

11. The lightning storm halted the transmission of our radio signals.

12. Purple is a mixture of blue and red; white or black can be added to increase the lightness or darkness of the hue.

13. Garth has an interest in magical potions.

14. He would like to master invisibility.

15. When Nelly moved forward, Fred fell backward.

Name: _____   **Date:** _____

You can figure out the meaning of unknown words by looking at the other words around them. If you need extra help—look the word up in the dictionary.

Directions: *Fill in the blanks using each word from the word bank only once.*

WORD BANK

wallet	token	worthwhile	wandered	policy
earned	bracelet	redeeming	pondered	ornate
occasion	gift	anticipation	balance	

Clara _____ about her mother's birthday for weeks. She wanted to buy

the perfect _____. Clara had saved most of her baby-sitting money for

this special _____. Clara _____ through many stores

at the mall, trying to find a meaningful _____ of her love. When she

walked inside the jewelry store, she immediately spotted what she wanted—an antique

gold _____; she knew her mother loved old, unique jewelry! The

bracelet cost $125. Clara counted every dollar in her _____ and realized

she was $50 short. A salesman told Clara about the store's layaway

_____, which meant Clara could pay for half of the bracelet now and the

other half when she _____ the rest of the payment.

That weekend, Clara made $16 for baby-sitting little Nelson, $9 for _____

empty soda cans and bottles she'd collected, and $25 for cutting two lawns. Excitedly,

Clara rode her bicycle to the jewelry store and gave the salesman the

_____ of the payment. He wrapped the bracelet in an

_____ pink box.

Monday was the big day. Clara's _____ nearly got the best of her, but it

was all _____! Clara's mother cried with joy when she opened the box.

Name: _____   **Date:** _____

The new girl in our class has a <u>dainty</u> manner.

    a. delicate   b. harsh

Everyone notices how hard Zachary works to <u>achieve</u> his goals.

    a. locate   b. reach

There is a <u>slim</u> chance that Samantha will be elected the new cheerleader alternate.

    a. no   b. slight

Our school nurse cannot <u>dispense</u> medication without a note from a doctor and a parent.

    a. distribute   b. hold

Mrs. Wright gave us a <u>verbal</u> pop quiz. We had to answer her questions out loud.

    a. oral   b. physical

Coach Enriquez <u>trains</u> the soccer team how to pass the ball.

    a. instruct   b. agree to

Sydney decided to <u>decline</u> the invitation to the fifth grade sleepover at Mary Ellen's.

    a. reject   b. special part of the year

The class assignment is to <u>capture</u> different kinds of bugs for study and identification.

    a. release   b. catch

Mr. Edwards has decided to <u>terminate</u> his teaching career at the end of this school year.

    a. begin   b. end

Mr. Edwards' <u>colleagues</u> are planning a retirement party in his honor.

    a. relatives   b. coworkers

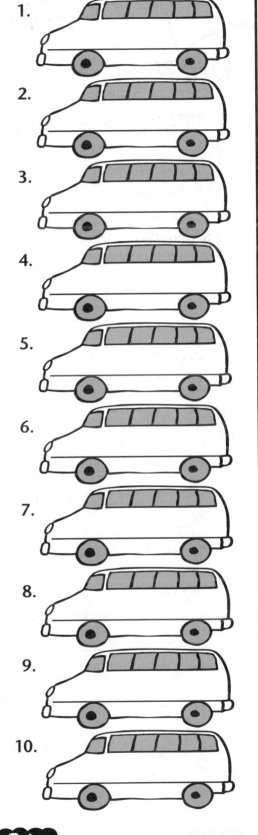

1.
2.
3.
4.
5.
6.
7.
8.
9.
10.

Name: _____   **Date:** _____

In three weeks, we are presenting a <u>recital</u> at school. Our band director can <u>appreciate</u> that we are nervous, since this is our first time playing in front of an audience.

1. recital	a. party	b. meeting	c. performance	d. dinner
2. appreciate	a. understand	b. misunderstand	c. motivate	d. observe

We <u>improvise</u> during many practice sessions, using a <u>variety</u> of notes and sounds. Then, we settle down and play some music everyone <u>recognizes</u>.

3. improvise	a. make up new parts	b. take turns	c. impress others	d. play show tunes
4. variety	a. a few	b. different and many	c. seven	d. one or two
5. recognizes	a. likes	b. hears	c. is familiar with	d. can dance to

The <u>instruments</u> in our band are different from one another. Some are <u>woodwinds</u>, like clarinets.

6. instruments	a. doctor's tools	b. used to make musical sounds	c. things used to cut	d. used by pilot's to navigate
7. woodwinds	a. played with a pick, bow or fingers	b. played with lips and breath	c. played with sticks	d. played when hammers strike a string

<u>String instruments</u>, like violins, are made of wood and have strings stretched across them. Percussion instruments, like drums, make noise when they are <u>struck</u> or shaken. Woodwind instruments, like the clarinet, <u>require</u> the player to blow into the instrument to make sound.

8. string instruments	a. played with a pick, bow or fingers	b. played with lips and breath	c. played with sticks	d. played when hammers strike a string
9. struck	a. hit	b. dropped	c. cracked	d. pushed
10. require	a. need	b. motivate	c. plan	d. teach

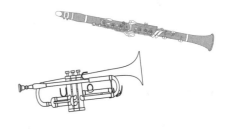

Name: _____   **Date:** _____

WORD BANK

peril	hazard	adequate	astonished
exclaimed	torment	pester	prehistoric
ripped	ancient	tore	inquire
whispered	question	sufficient	amazed

1. "Let go of my harmonica," I <u>said</u>.

_____   _____

2. If you <u>bother</u> my little sister, she'll bite you.

_____   _____

3. Please <u>ask</u> your mom if she knows how to remove gum from hair.

_____   _____

4. When gym socks get <u>old</u> they smell like you just wore them even if they're washed.

_____   _____

5. Are there <u>enough</u> chairs for the guests?

_____   _____

6. Liz has a <u>surprised</u> look on her face.

_____   _____

7. The detective was in great <u>danger</u>.

_____   _____

8. Casey was so embarrassed when his shorts <u>split</u>!

_____   _____

Once you read vocabulary clues and consider all the facts (even picture clues), you can draw a conclusion about what you've read—that's called an inference.

Directions: *Guess the ocean creature by reading the vocabulary clues below. Write the answer on the line. Then draw the underwater creature in the ocean scene below.*

1. Reptile with flippers; lays its eggs in the sand: _____

2. Immense ocean mammal, with a blow spout: _____

3. Stinging umbrella-like jelly creature: _____

4. A creature that has five or more arms and is usually found in the shape of a star, able to bore holes in clam and oyster shells: _____

5. Comes in many varieties, including: great white, tiger, and sand: _____

6. Orange shellfish has two pincers and crawls on the ocean floor: _____

7. Underwater horse: _____

8. Also called a "sea cow": _____

Name: _____   **Date:** _____

1.

2.

3.

4.

5.

6.

1. _____
   _____

2. _____
   _____

3. _____
   _____

3. _____
   _____

4. _____
   _____

5. _____
   _____

6. _____
   _____

Name: _____   **Date:** _____

Words, words, words—It's not the word but how you use it that gives it meaning.

Directions: *Choose the word that belongs in both sentences. Then, write the word on the lines.*

1. My brother is practicing to be a drummer in a _____ band.
   Our neighbor threw a _____ at my brother while he was practicing the drums.

jazz	kiss	rubber	rock

2. People of every _____ should be treated with respect.
   He led for most of the _____ and then tired.

journey	religion	race	contest

3. Elephants use their _____ to help clear the forest.
   I always carry a spare tire in the _____ of my car.

wheel	trunk	tusks	boot

4. The game of _____ is very popular in England.
   Jamie always forgets to look before he _____ across the road.

soccer	dashes	scurries	darts

5. My dog constantly jumps our _____.
   The thief took the stolen goods to a _____.

fence	salesman	gate	keeper

6. It was peaceful watching as the cows _____ on the grass in the meadow.
   Her hand lightly _____ his cheek as she brushed away the flies.

browsed	caressed	grazed	touched

7. We will have to _____ the pool to repair the plaster on the bottom.
   The children are afraid to go into the _____ house next door.

hollow	drain	empty	vacant

8. The _____ on this ancient monument is very hard to read.
   Have you read the _____ about the mermaid and the dolphin?

myth	legend	motto	inscription

9. When monkeys find a tree full of ripe fruit they _____ themselves.
   There is a large _____ between us and our destination.

ravine	gorge	stuff	canyon

10. While we were hiking we found an old _____ up on that hill.
    Our club has a very _____ situation to discuss at our next meeting.

burial mound	solemn	mine	grave

11. My sister is the best _____ on her softball team.
    A cool _____ of lemonade is always welcome on a hot day.

player	quart	pitcher	glass

Name: _____   **Date:** _____

Meanings

1. slang for dollar
2. yelp
3. fruit pie with one crust
4. gherkin
5. beverage
6. disclose, reveal
7. squeeze
8. hot dog
9. conifer tree
10. magical influence
11. predicament
12. trail following ship
13. crack; become rough
14. leave helpless
15. musical tone
16. bold talk
17. male deer
18. hit
19. emergency
20. skin of a tree
21. mope, long for
22. one who mends shoes
23. boy or man
24. naked
25. thread of string
26. stop sleeping
27. say the letters of a word
28. throw

Words With More Than One Meaning

A. pine |___| or |___|

B. chap |___| or |___|

C. buck |___| or |___|

D. pinch |___| or |___|

E. cobbler |___| or |___|

F. frank |___| or |___|

G. punch |___| or |___|

H. spell |___| or |___|

I. bark |___| or |___|

J. wake |___| or |___|

K. strand |___| or |___|

L. pitch |___| or |___|

M. bare |___| or |___|

N. pickle |___| or |___|

An author uses signal words to tell you how to read. Signal words help you understand how information is organized and provide clues about what is important.

Directions: *Write the signal words and phrases under the correct heading.*

otherwise

when

such as

finally

for example

lately

specifically

rather

but

however

once

much like

even though

immediately

similar to

Sequence and Time Signals
(Order and time of ideas.)
Example: <u>Before</u> each meal, I choose something healthy to eat.

1. _____
2. _____
3. _____
4. _____
5. _____

Illustration Signals
(Here's what the idea means.)
Example: <u>For instance</u>, I always include a fruit in my meals.

1. _____
2. _____
3. _____
4. _____
5. _____

Change of Direction Signals
(We're doubling back on this idea.)
Example: <u>Although</u>, I should be adding more vegetables to my meals, too

1. _____
2. _____
3. _____
4. _____
5. _____

Name: _____   **Date:** _____

Find and circle all the sequence and time signal words in the story below. Then, write what happens in the story next to each signal word below. Finally, draw a picture to illustrate the story on the back of this page.

Many kids have fish or cats or parakeets for pets, but I prefer to have a blue-tailed, lizard-scaled, fire-breathing dragon. Initially, when I laid eyes on Smokey, I was more than a bit scared. Terrified is a better adjective to describe the angst in my gut. Smokey has piercing red eyes and teeth sharper than any razor or dagger edge. Next, I assumed my life was about to go up in flames. But then he smiled at me and blew a few puffs of harmless smoke. After that, my fear subsided and we became instant friends. Dad said I could keep Smokey as long as he didn't set fire to the house.

Smokey and I have lots of fun roaming the seven seas together, with me perched high upon his crooked tail. At night he sleeps under the huge magnolia tree in our yard. However, nosy Mrs. Dullpepper got uptight when she learned I had a pet dragon. I was going to have Smokey warm her up a little, but Dad forbid it. Then I got a great idea. Smokey and I went door to door to share his services as a barbecue starter. His fire is so strong he can start a blaze from fifty yards. Finally, everyone agreed that Smokey was a fine neighbor. Smokey and I spent a lot of the summer at barbecues, until we decided to start charging for services. Funny, no one wanted to pay. That's just as well. Chasing pirates across the seven seas is more fun anyway!

Initially: _____

_____

_____

Next: _____

_____

_____

After that:_____

_____

_____

Then:_____

_____

_____

Finally:_____

_____

_____

Name: _____ **Date:** _____

Hey, first let me introduce myself. My name is B.B. Wolf. Now, many of you have heard of me before. I got mixed up with that little girl with the red hood. Everyone believed her sappy, one-sided tale. As if I would want a basket full of bland cookies—whoever heard of cookies without chocolate chips?

When the "real" story gets out about what happened that day in the forest, suddenly I'll be the most famous canine in the world! I can see it now; immediately I'll be mobbed by fans and photographers—much like a movie star. I'll have to lurk around corners and wear dark glasses when I go out.

However, once that crazy kid gets her story straight, I must admit I will enjoy being famous. At last everyone will know the hero I was that day, gallantly escorting Red and her yucky cookies through the dangerous forest to Grandma's house. Finally, it will be cleared up once and for all that I do not wear Grandma clothes! At last I will be able to enjoy the recognition and fame I deserve.

_____

_____

_____

_____

_____

_____

_____

_____

_____

_____

_____

_____

Name: _____ **Date:** _____

Become best friends with your dictionary and glossary. They can help you sort out the meaning of all kinds of words.

Directions: *Do this activity alone or with a partner. Circle the correct definition of the words listed below. Use a dictionary to check your answers.*

1. **squab**
   a. a sailor
   b. a baby pigeon
   c. someone who doesn't clean their room

2. **vertical**
   a. upright, or straight up and down
   b. a calorie-free vegetable drink
   c. inside out

3. **cylinder**
   a. a document that keeps track of months and weeks
   b. a tube
   c. the middle of your shoe

4. **harsh**
   a. to be quiet
   b. cruel
   c. soft and smooth

5. **lope**
   a. run
   b. a long rope
   c. someone who doesn't know much

6. **croon**
   a. sing
   b. scratch an itch
   c. a large yellow bird

7. **smirk**
   a. the sound a fly makes when it hits the swatter
   b. smile
   c. a little blue creature

8. **ambidextrous**
   a. able to climb ceilings
   b. to be both left- and right-handed
   c. a two-legged dinosaur

9. **omit**
   a. to leave out
   b. a bad odor
   c. a prophecy

10. **jinx**
    a. game using jacks and marbles
    b. a type of wild cat
    c. a curse

11. **mutation**
    a. variation
    b. alien
    c. small mammal

12. **indication**
    a. average
    b. clue
    c. cheat

13. **fluster**
    a. mass of bubbles
    b. sweep
    c. upset

14. **compensate**
    a. accomplish
    b. make proper payment
    c. unsettle

15. **ravenous**
    a. very hungry
    b. enough
    c. villain

 Name: _____

Date: _____

Directions: Read what a dictionary entry tells you. Then, use the dictionary entries to answer the questions below.

What does a dictionary entry tell you?

It tells you the spelling of a word.

It tells you how to pronounce the word.

It tells you how the word is divided into syllables.

friction (frik-shuhn) 1: rubbing. *Friction causes heat.* 2: force that slows down objects when they rub against each other. 3: disagreement or anger. *There was much friction between the two teams.*

handle (han-duhl) 1: part of an object that you use to carry, move, or hold that object, as in a door handle. 2: pick something up in your hands in order to look at it carefully. *The sign in the stores said, "Please handle the china with care."* 3: deal with someone or something. *Carol is very good at handling tricky situations.*

It tells you the meaning of the word. If the word has more than one meaning, each definition will be numbered.

It tells you how the word is used in the examples that follow the definition.

1. How many syllables are in the word friction? _____

2. How many syllables are in the word handle? _____

3. Divide handle into syllables. _____

4. What is the phonetic spelling for friction? _____

5. What is the phonetic for handle? _____

6. Which syllable in handle is emphasized? _____

7. How many definitions are listed for friction? _____

8. How many definitions are listed for handle? _____

_____ a. The handle on my purse is broken.

_____ b. There is a lot of friction between Pete and Marcus.

_____ c. Rubbing your hands together quickly creates heated friction.

_____ d. Please handle the antique vase carefully.

_____ e. Let Tom handle the situation, he knows what to do.

_____ f. The friction caused by the gears rubbing against each other slowed down the machine.

Name: _____   **Date:** _____

King Tutankhamen

King Tutankhamen was only nineteen when he died. It is thought that his enemies murdered him. Compared to other Pharaohs, his tomb was modest.

Ancient Egyptians believed their Pharaohs to be gods. When they died, Pharaohs were carefully embalmed. This preserved the King's body. The mummified corpses were put away in fancy tombs and surrounded with all the things they would need in the afterlife. The tombs were then carefully sealed. Egypt's best builders designed the tombs to keep out thieves. In some cases, heavy boulders were used to block passageways. Sometimes false doorways and hidden rooms were designed to confuse robbers. Finally, a curse was placed on the entrance.

Most of these precautions failed. In ancient times grave robbers found their way into the tombs. They unsealed the doors, hammered their way around the boulders and found the secrets of the hidden rooms. No one knows for sure if any of the thieves suffered from the wrath of a curse. However, many legends say they did.

Glossary

Ancient: _____

_____

_____

Corpse:_____

_____

_____

Curse: _____

_____

_____

Embalm: _____

_____

_____

Legend: _____

_____

Pharaoh: _____

_____

Revenge: _____

_____

_____

Tomb: _____

_____

_____

Wrath: _____

_____

_____

Name: _____   Date: _____

Words are such fun. Check this out! Synonyms = words with similar meanings; Antonyms = words with opposite meanings; Homophones = words that sound the same but have different meanings and usually different spellings.

Directions: *Replace the underlined common word with a synonym from the word box. Write the new sentence on the line below.*

pleasant	sprinted	grave	enormous	trounced
impolite	declared	cease	tiny	fine

1. The Sharks <u>beat</u> the Bombers in overtime.

   _____

2. Jennifer <u>said</u> that I am her best friend.

   _____

3. Luke <u>ran</u> all the way home from school.

   _____

4. Walter's pet snake is <u>big</u>.

   _____

5. My pesky little sister would not <u>stop</u> picking up the phone while I was talking!

   _____

6. Max has a <u>small</u> scar above his right eye. He's so handsome!

   _____

7. Mrs. Hoofer is a <u>nice</u> teacher.

   _____

8. I did a <u>good</u> job on my science report.

   _____

9. Mr. Potter said there would be <u>serious</u> consequences if I failed another test.

   _____

10. Kim insisted it was <u>rude</u> of me to splash her at the water fountain.

   _____

Name: _____   **Date:** _____

shorten	brave	supported	stupid
fantasy	terrible	enemies	discontinue
secure	tame	marvelous	never

1. Hector is a <u>great</u> acrobat. You should see him do a somersault!

_____

2. Melissa <u>always</u> puts on sunscreen before going to the beach.

_____

3. That ladder is <u>unstable</u>.

_____

4. I asked Aunt Tilley if she could please <u>extend</u> her visit.

_____

5. Rick and Fred have been <u>allies</u> since the last football game.

_____

6. I think the story Rita told was absolute <u>fact</u>!

_____

7. Joe <u>betrayed</u> his class when the teacher asked who thought she should assign weekend homework.

_____

8. I have the world's most <u>cowardly</u> dog!

_____

9. Jessica plans to <u>maintain</u> her ballet lessons.

_____

10. I hope I did not insult anyone with my <u>intelligent</u> joke.

_____

11. After the first drop, the roller coaster ride was really <u>wild</u>.

_____

12. We had a <u>terrible</u> time at the amusement park.

_____

Name: _____ **Date:** _____

1. "I have money _____," said Wally. "I'll pay the _____ dollars if you come _____ the show with me."

   | to | too | two |

2. The reporter asked me _____ or not I liked the _____ in Florida.

   | weather | whether |

3. Dad was excited when he heard there was a _____ on _____ boats. Mom didn't seem as excited.

   | sail | sale |

4. If I have _____ this week I'm going to plant _____ in my herb garden.

   | thyme | time |

5. Kevin is looking very _____ after eating ten super burgers. Maybe he should sleep with a _____ next to his bed.

   | pail | pale |

6. _____ meeting with _____ advisors over _____.

   | their | they're | there |

7. The wedding will take place on a remote _____. _____ be walking the bride down the _____.

   | aisle | I'll | isle |

8. I was sick at home with the _____. Just as I was about to light a fire, a bird _____ down the fireplace _____.

   | flew | flu | flue |

1. market
2. bad
3. golden
4. military rank
5. scatter
6. insect
7. grain of corn
8. worship
9. run away
10. odd
11. bird
12. pay out
13. award
14. opposite of innocence
15. interfere
16. complaining sound
17. drink
18. prey

a. ☐ bizarre
b. ☐ kernel
c. ☐ flea
d. ☐ disperse
e. ☐ whine
f. ☐ bazaar
g. ☐ foul
h. ☐ gilt
i. ☐ pray
j. ☐ medal
k. ☐ wine
l. ☐ disburse
m. ☐ flee
n. ☐ colonel
o. ☐ fowl
p. ☐ guilt
q. ☐ victim
r. ☐ meddle

You must be a good reader to correctly follow directions. Pay attention to the details.

Directions: *Study the map. Then, find the shortest directions to each point and answer the questions. Remember to use the compass rose.*

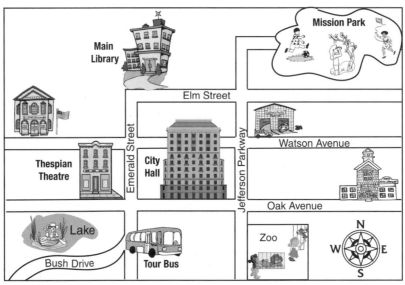

1. What is the shortest travel route from Thespian Theatre to Mission Park? _____
   _____

2. What is the shortest route to get to the Zoo from City Hall? _____

3. Would you travel north or south if you wanted to get to the Lake from the Main Library?
   _____

4. What is the name of the street directly in front of City Hall? What direction does it run?
   _____

5. What two streets are named after presidents? _____

6. What direction do the two streets named after trees run? _____

7. What natural landmark does the tour bus pass as it travels south on Emerald Street?
   _____

8. What building is at the northwest corner of Elm and Emerald Streets? _____

9. If you travel east on Watson Avenue and south on Jefferson Parkway, where will you end up?
   _____

10. If the tour bus turns around and travels north on Emerald Street and east to the center of
    Oak Avenue, what is the name of the building the bus will be in front of? _____
    _____

Name: _____   **Date:** _____

Sunny-Seed Cookies

Ingredients

- 1 cup butter or shortening
- 1 cup brown sugar (firmly packed)
- 1 cup granulated sugar
- 2 eggs
- 1 teaspoon vanilla
- $1\frac{1}{2}$ cup unsifted regular flour
- $\frac{1}{2}$ teaspoon salt
- 1 teaspoon baking soda
- 3 cups rolled oats
- 1 jar dry roasted sunflower seeds (shelled)

Steps to Follow

1. Cream together butter, brown sugar, and granulated sugar.
2. Add eggs and vanilla, and beat to blend.
3. Add flour, salt, soda, oats, and mix thoroughly.
4. Gently blend in sunflower seeds.
5. Form dough into long rolls, about $1\frac{1}{2}$" in diameter. Wrap in clear plastic film and chill thoroughly.
6. Slice dough into $\frac{1}{4}$" thick slices.
7. Arrange on an ungreased cookie sheet and bake at 350 degrees for 8 to 10 minutes.
8. Cool on wire racks and store airtight. Makes 9 dozen.

a. How many cookies does this recipe make? _____

b. What is the second step? _____

c. What is the fourth step? _____

d. What kind of seeds do you need for this recipe? _____

e. What would you use to cut the cookies into slices? _____

f. What are the types of sugar needed in the recipe? _____

_____

g. What would happen if you left out the seeds? _____

h. What is the second to last step? _____

i. What would you need to do if you wanted to serve these cookies to 216 people? _____

_____

Name: _____ **Date:** _____

Classifying is an important scientific procedure. It's putting things into groups according to their characteristics.

Directions: *Write each characteristic of animals in the left shape, the characteristic of plants in the right shape, and characteristic of both animals and plants in the space where the two shapes overlap.*

Need shelter	Have roots
Eat meat and/or plants	Can be eaten by humans
Are able to move	Reproduce
Need water to survive	Need air to survive
Make their own food	Grow
Turn sunlight into energy	Eliminate waste from their bodies

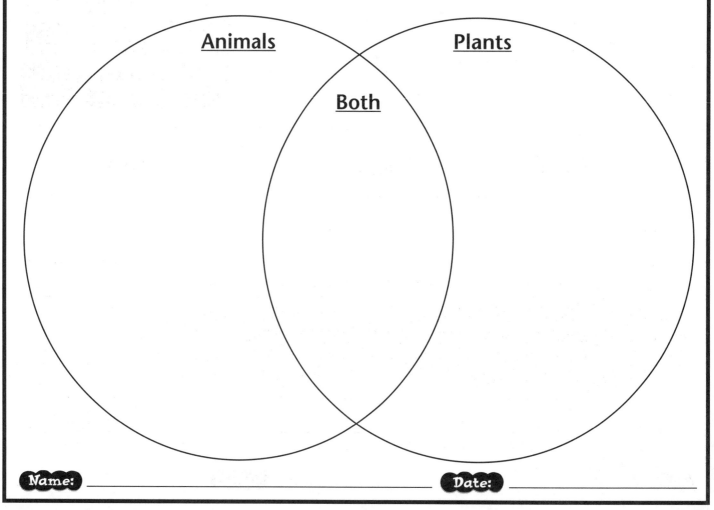

Animals   **Plants**

Both

I have my very own garden
I tend to it every day
There's thyme, cantaloupe, chives, and asparagus
Delicious in their own way.

Watermelon, basil, dates, and beans:
Waxed, lima, string, and French
Red potatoes, strawberry, and grape vines above and down below
I admire them from my bench!

Green tomatoes, radicchio, and apples the size of moons
Hot peppers, sweet peppers, and yellow peppers bloom
Nectarines, peaches, and bananas
Keep me busy until harvest—July, August, and June!

Fruits	**Vegetables**	**Herbs**

Name: _____   Date: _____

Analogies, metaphors, and similes are words or groups of words that are like a puzzle. You really need to think about what the words are telling you to get the big picture.

Directions: Analyze the relationship between the first two words before you shade in the circle in front of the correct analogy.

1. *easy* is to *simple* as *hard* is to

| ○ solid | ○ difficult |

2. *cabin* is to *build* as *well* is to

| ○ dig | ○ water |

3. *sing* is to *pleased* as *shout* is to

| ○ yell | ○ angry |

4. *book* is to *character* as *recipe* is to

| ○ ingredient | ○ food |

5. *engine* is to *go* as *break* is to

| ○ move | ○ stop |

6. *length* is to *weight* as *inches* is to

| ○ pound | ○ yard |

7. *princess* is to *queen* as *prince* is to

| ○ royalty | ○ king |

8. *tree* is to *lumber* as *wheat* is to

| ○ flour | ○ bread |

9. *cell* is to *skin* as *brick* is to

| ○ mortar | ○ wall |

10. *carpenter* is to *house* as *composer* is to

| ○ symphony | ○ marching band |

11. *silk* is to *smooth* as *sandpaper* is to

| ○ rough | ○ sand |

12. *bear* is to *den* as *bee* is to

| ○ flower | ○ hive |

13. *bat* is to *baseball* as *whistle* is to

| ○ vendor | ○ referee |

14. *five* is to *fifteen* as *three* is to

| ○ twelve | ○ nine |

Name: _____ Date: _____

Reading Comprehension • Saddleback Publishing, Inc. ©2002   3 Watson, Irvine, CA 92618•Phone (888)SDL-BACK• www.sdlback.com

Example:
Ann is a walking encyclopedia.
Ann is very smart and knows a lot about many different topics.

1. That car is an old dinosaur.
   _____
   _____

2. Jealousy is a green-eyed monster.
   _____
   _____

3. She is a regular adding machine.
   _____
   _____

4. At night my bedroom is a real icebox.
   _____
   _____

5. His stomach is a bottomless pit.
   _____
   _____

6. He turned thumbs down at the idea of transferring to a new school.
   _____
   _____

7. The baby was a clinging vine near his mother.
   _____
   _____

8. Judy is a snail when it comes to getting her work done.
   _____
   _____

9. Mr. Wheeler's bark is worse than his bite.
   _____
   _____

10. He is faster than a streak of lightening.
    _____
    _____

Name: _____ **Date:** _____

Example:
Similes describe a person, place, thing, or action with colorful or visual words.
Simile: Sam is eating like it is going out of style!
Translation: *Sam is eating a lot and he is eating very quickly.*

It was raining cats and dogs and foolish Ralph had left his jacket in the park. "You are dumber than a post!" teased Ralph's sister Sarah. "But my love for you is like a red, red, rose. So, I'll help you find your jacket in the rain! Anyway, it has the house keys in the pocket and I would welcome shelter—I'm soaked like a sponge."

Ralph and Sarah raced between the raindrops toward the park to look for the jacket. Neither of them had eaten since lunch, and they were feeling as weak as a kitten "I'm so hungry I could eat a horse," moaned Ralph.

"I feel like a wet rag," said Sarah, wiping the rain from her face. "If you would have given me the keys like I asked, we wouldn't be in this pickle!" Ralph felt bad. He knew Sarah was right. He should have given her the keys an hour ago when she wanted to go home. Instead, he played the bossy big brother and made her wait. Just as they reached the park, the heavens opened! Ralph spotted his jacket and grabbed it before a big gust of wind could send it sailing. Ralph and Sarah ran home as fast as they could. Their mother was waiting for them at the door with dry towels and hot chocolate. She'd gotten home from work early. Ralph gave Sarah a sarcastic grin.

"Don't even say it!" warned Sarah. "Or I'll be tempted to beat you like a drum!" They both started to laugh.

1. Simile:_____

   Translation:_____

2. Simile:_____

   Translation:_____

3. Simile:_____

   Translation:_____

4. Simile:_____

   Translation:_____

Name: _____   **Date:** _____

1. As big as a house
2. Under the weather
3. Stop on a dime
4. As old as the hills
5. Money doesn't grow on trees
6. As sly as a fox
7. As quick as a bunny
8. As free as a bird

Garth Gantuan was ⭕ <u>a large man</u>. He was the largest man in Flogenville and though you wouldn't guess by looking at his massive frame, Garth was also ⭕ <u>a very fast runner.</u> Garth was married to Maben Sue; her daddy was the richest man in Flogenville and as such, Maben Sue never learned ⭕ <u>you had to work to earn money.</u>

One day Garth arrived home after a hard day's work at the factory in Flogenville to find his dear bride soggy with tears. "What's the matter, my sugar plum?" cooed Garth, wrapping his massive hands around his wife to comfort her.

⭕ "<u>I'm not feeling well,</u>" she sniffled. There is a contest being held to see who is the best runner in the state. The winner gets a new convertible car. I need that car so I can feel better—you see I need to ⭕ <u>get out of here</u>." Maben Sue was using an ⭕ <u>ancient</u> female family device—tears—to get Garth to race and win her the car. She could start them up or make them ⭕ <u>cease</u>, at will.

"Unconfined, my darling, I didn't know you felt that way. Of course I will win you the car. Whatever it takes to make you happy." Garth truly loved his wife, and Maben Sue didn't give it a thought that Garth might suspect her of being ⭕ <u>cunning</u>.

The race was set for the following Saturday. When the gun sounded, Garth took off with a blast. Faster and faster he ran until the spectators could see only a speck in the distance. Maben Sue was presented the car. Though no one ever heard from Garth again. Some say he just finally got smart and ran away from Maben Sue.

Name: _____ **Date:** _____

Categories put information neatly into place.

Directions: *Put the following items in the correct categories.*

Hurricane Fred howled through town like a coyote with water wings. Trees toppled, cars careened, and stuff at the Oinkity-Boinkity convenience market was scattered and tossed—making chaos out of things! Help manager Johnny put the items back in the correct aisle. Without your assistance, he may be at this task for a very long while!

Aisle 1—Canned Goods: _____

_____

_____

Aisle 2—Fruits & Vegetables: _____

_____

_____

Aisle 3—Pet Food: _____

_____

_____

Aisle 4—Dairy: _____

_____

_____

Aisle 5—Boxed Foods: _____

_____

_____

Name: _____   Date: _____

It was midnight when I got the call on my purple, pocket cell phone, which I always leave positioned on my nightstand. The ring jolted me out of bed. Grabbing my flannel footed-pajama bottoms, I answered the phone. It was my neighbor, Mrs. Hooper; she was hysterical. I could barely make out what she was saying amid the ranting sobs. It sounded something like, "I'm a hog sissy."

"Well, Mrs. Hooper, that may be true, but isn't it an odd hour of the night to call me with such a confession?" I rubbed the sleep out of my ears and listened harder.

"My dog's missing!" She repeated...actually, squealed. "You must find him immediately. I will pay you $100." Money appeals to my sympathetic side—so I threw a gray trench coat over my pajamas and headed out the door. I was at Mrs. Hooper's house in 1.4 minutes.

"Where did you last see the canine?" I inquired, already canvassing the room for clues.

"Snuggles was next to me on the pillow when I fell asleep at exactly 11:47. There was a loud sawing noise and I awoke with a start—I noticed Snuggles was gone. I was terrified. I panicked. That's when I called you at precisely midnight."

"Hmmmmm," I thought, "Time is important here...not much passed between the time she fell asleep and then awoke and called me. On top of that we need to consider the loud sawing noise. Dogs have sensitive ears." I summoned up the courage to ask a pivotal question. "Mrs. Hooper, don't take this the wrong way, but do you snore?" She blushed. "I thought so. Let's have a look in your closet." As I suspected, there was Snuggles under a pile of dirty laundry—his paws tightly covering his ears.

The reunion was swift and I was back in bed within the hour, $100 bill firmly clenched in my hand. Sweet dreams followed.

Important facts: *List five facts that are relevant to solving the case.*

_____

_____

_____

_____

_____

Unimportant facts: *List five pieces of information that have no bearing on the case.*

_____

_____

_____

_____

_____

Things that are the similar can also be different.

Directions: Examine the two buildings below. Describe how they are the same and how are they different.

School House

Light House

Same: _____

_____

_____

_____

_____

_____

Different: _____

_____

_____

_____

_____

_____

Name: _____   **Date:** _____

Greetings from the windy city of Chicago, situated on beautiful Lake Michigan! Sorry for the delay in writing but my computer is on the blink since the movers dropped it. My e-mail isn't functioning properly; as a result, I must resort to snail mail. There are many other bummers I have to deal with since leaving you in Malibu—the most difficult is not waking up in the morning to a pristine view of the Pacific Ocean. The lake is magnificent, but there aren't any handsome surfers, tanned lifeguards, or compelling reasons to put on my new bikini—just sailboats and gray skies.

I like my new school, but the kids don't dress as stylishly as they do at Malibu Elementary. Maybe because uniforms are required! Every student wears the same ugly green plaid vest and either pants or a skirt. I'd rather wear a skirt, but it's just been too darn cold to show off my tan legs.

We also start school earlier here, at 7:55 a. m., so I'm usually either sleepy or late to school. I liked it better in California with school starting at 8:25 a.m. Instead of a snack recess, we go straight through the morning and are allowed more time for lunch recess. If you live near school, you're even allowed to go home for lunch!

Kids like to play tetherball at my new school. I'm a spaz at tetherball. Looks like this handball champion has a lot of practicing to do! After school, most of the kids take the bus home instead of walking like we used to. I guess that's because it rains and snows a lot in Chicago, unlike sunny Malibu! I miss attending our scouting meetings and tennis practice. My mom said she is going to enroll me in singing lessons. Doesn't that sound neat? Britney Spears, watch out!

Well, I hope you are doing well back in Malibu. I miss you so much. When do you think you can come for a visit? June? Well, until then, let's not forget to wear the friendship bracelets we made for each other. I wear mine every day!

Miss you,
Shelby

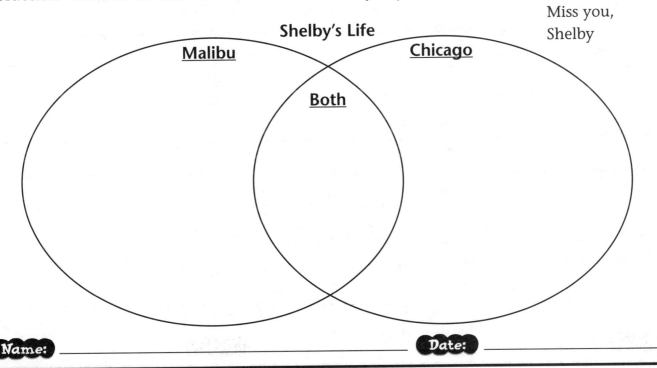

Shelby's Life

Malibu   Chicago

Both

When looking for information, sometimes the questions are as important as the answers.

Directions: *Below you will find answers and hints. Refer to an encyclopedia and then write an interesting and detailed question that would logically lead you to the given answer. The first one is done for you.*

1. **Answer: Napoleon Bonaparte (French History)**
   Question: Who is famous for his defeat at Waterloo and for marrying Josephine?

2. **Answer: Marsupial (Animals)**
   Question: _____
   _____

3. **Answer: Frank Lloyd Wright (Architecture)**
   Question: _____
   _____

4. **Answer: Henry Ford (Famous American)**
   Question: _____
   _____

5. **Answer: Gettysburg (Civil War)**
   Question: _____
   _____

6. **Answer: Incas (South America)**
   Question: _____
   _____

7. **Answer: Harry Potter (Literature)**
   Question: _____
   _____

8. **Answer: Shakespeare (British Theater)**
   Question: _____
   _____

9. **Answer: Planetarium (Science)**
   Question: _____
   _____

10. **Answer: Jousting (History & Sports)**
    Question: _____
    _____

Name: _____   **Date:** _____

Find a friend, classmate, family member, or neighbor who is willing to be interviewed. Think about some important questions that you will need answered in order to write a good biography. Write these questions on the lines provided. Then on the back of the paper, put the answers together into a story.

Childhood questions:

1. _____?
2. _____?
3. _____?

Personal background questions:

1. _____?
2. _____?
3. _____?

Likes and dislikes questions:

1. _____?
2. _____?
3. _____?

Questions about future goals:

1. _____?
2. _____?
3. _____?

Name: _____   **Date:** _____

Hey Smartie! Idioms are groups of words that have a different meaning compared to the other words in a passage.

Directions: *Define the underlined idioms on the lines below. Use the back of this page as needed.*

Jacob's tennis match was to begin in an hour. He had <u>massive butterflies in his stomach</u>. He decided to take a walk in the woods near his house. Suddenly, he saw a black and white face peeking out from behind a bush. Realizing that it was a skunk, Jacob ran, but the skunk <u>followed in hot pursuit</u>. Jacob <u>stepped on the gas</u>, faked to the left, and sprinted the other way. But it was too late—the skunk beat Jacob home.

"Go away you pesky skunk!" whispered Jacob to his new shadow, not wanting to warrant a spraying. "I have to get ready for my match, and I don't need a stinky mascot."

"Oh, if it's not Jacob, <u>running off at the mouth</u> as usual. Who are you talking too?" It was Drake Malfog, Jacob's opponent and least favorite person. Jacob wanted to scream something rude at Drake, but he didn't want to startle the skunk. "<u>Cat got your tongue</u>, Jacob? Well, see you on the tennis court, when I <u>whip you into shape</u>." When Jacob looked back the skunk was out of sight. Jacob was relieved and hurried into the house, grabbed his gear, and headed to the tennis courts.

City stadium was <u>busting at the seams</u>. Drake was already on the tennis court. Jacob won the toss and picked up a ball to serve, he began to sneeze and his eyes burned. Someone had sprinkled the balls with hot pepper. "Need a tissue?" yelled Drake from across the court. Jacob was about to protest when he saw a now familiar sight—that little skunk directly behind Drake. Jacob decided to <u>let nature run it course</u> and served the ball.

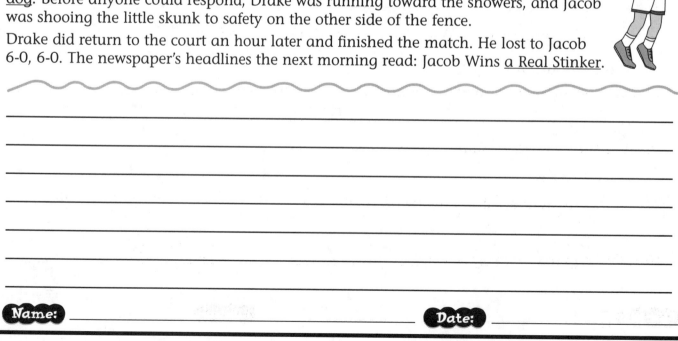

A smell like no other immediately filled the air surrounding Drake Malfog. "A skunk!" shouted Drake. "I've been sprayed!" he moaned, <u>chasing himself in circles like a rabid dog</u>. Before anyone could respond, Drake was running toward the showers, and Jacob was shooing the little skunk to safety on the other side of the fence.

Drake did return to the court an hour later and finished the match. He lost to Jacob 6-0, 6-0. The newspaper's headlines the next morning read: Jacob Wins <u>a Real Stinker</u>.

_____

_____

_____

_____

_____

_____

_____

Name: _____ **Date:** _____

killed two birds with one stone   barnburner

let the cat out of the bag   don't let the bedbugs bite

bull by the horns   tongue-tie

something the cat dragged in   busy as a bee

the straw that broke the camel's back   under the weather

1. Sarah's been as _____ today getting ready for her trip to Aruba.

2. Kevin _____ when he turned in his election speech for an English class assignment.

3. My mother always says the same thing when she tucks me in, "Goodnight, sleep tight; _____!"

4. Ryan took the _____ and gave his team a much-needed pep talk.

5. When Billy threw the spitball that hit Mrs. Turner, it was _____ _____.

6. After running home in the rain without an umbrella, I looked like _____."

7. When Rick didn't respond, his brother asked him, "What's wrong? Are you _____?"

8. Jane knew about her surprise party because Austin _____.

9. The sportscaster predicted the game would be a _____.

10. I woke up this morning feeling _____.

A newspaper article always tells the reader about each of the 5 W's.

WHO: 500 people attended from the town of Glendale
WHAT: Carter Family Circus of Animals and Acrobats
WHERE: Glendale Community Center
WHEN: Saturday, September 18th from 12:00 to 4:30 p.m.
WHY: The circus is in Glendale to raise money for the children's hospital.

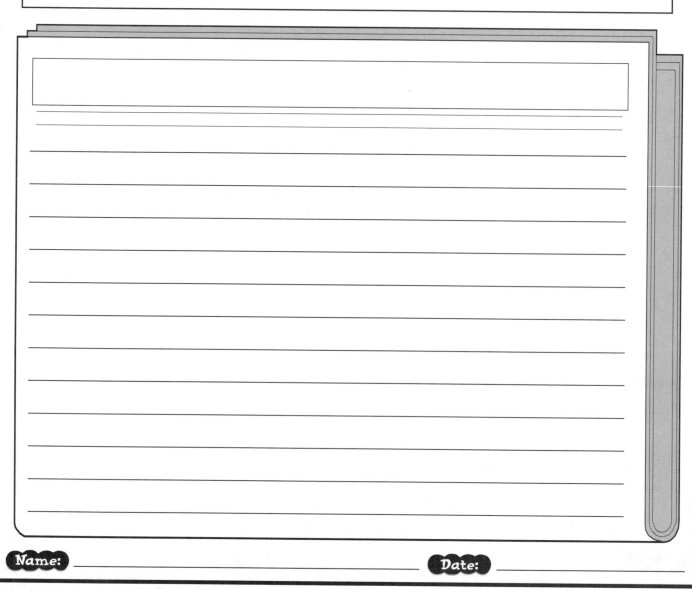

Name: _____

Date: _____

Virgo Horoscope

June will fulfill your wildest expectations for success, love, and money! You will now see rewards for every extra mile you've walked over the last few years. This is a great month because you will see your name in big letters and lights, dear Virgo. What a marvelous opportunity for reaching your goals and achieving your dreams—no matter how big you were dreaming, they will soon come true! All this good fortune will become apparent on June 22, your luckiest day of the month. You will find the most success in areas related to publishing, the Internet, telecommunications, computers, and software.

1. Who is the horoscope for? _____

_____

2. What month is being predicted? _____

_____

3. When is the luckiest day of the month? _____

_____

4. Where is the greatest success to be found? _____

_____

5. Why is this a great month? _____

_____

_____

_____

_____

_____

_____

_____

_____

Hmm.... predictions are fun. Predicting is guessing what things are about to happen using a few facts.

Directions: *Look at these book covers and read the titles. Predict what the books will be about on the lines provided. When you finish, read the jacket summaries and check whether or not your predictions were correct.*

The Traveling Trio
Orphans on a Mission

Book Summary: The Traveling Trio is the story of three kids who run away from a mean foster home in search of a better life and adventure. Fate has it that their paths cross with millionaire, Dexter Dollars, a former orphan, in New York's Kennedy Airport. Dexter decides to give the boys his luxury jet and a task. The task teaches the boys life lessons and gives them an adventure they will never forget. Will the boys complete the task? What is the wonderful reward Dexter promises them if they succeed? This is such a riveting novel you won't put it down until the last word is read!

1. My prediction:_____
    My prediction was   correct   incorrect

Who was Leonardo da Vinci?

Book Summary: Who was Leonardo da Vinci? He had a keen eye and quick mind that led him to make important scientific discoveries, yet he never published his ideas. He was a gentle vegetarian who loved animals and despised war, yet he worked as a military engineer to invent advanced and deadly weapons. He was one of the greatest painters of the Italian Renaissance, yet he left only a handful of completed paintings.

2. My prediction:_____
    My prediction was   correct   incorrect

Drools and Creepers
Unlikely Crime Fighters

Book Summary: Drools and Creepers are the unlikeliest pair of detectives ever to scratch a flea. When the Flick family fortune is stolen from behind their fake fireplace, this dog and cat team up and use their animal smarts to help the Flick family get back what is rightfully theirs—and a whole lot more! Drools and Creepers uncover a surprising mystery that leads to an amazing discovery and fortune.

3. My prediction:_____
    My prediction was   correct   incorrect

Name: _____   **Date:** _____

1. Omar doesn't notice that his soda can has sprung a leak. He puts the can into his backpack and heads off to school. Omar's English report is in his backpack.

   _____

   _____

   _____

   _____

2. Jennifer finishes addressing all 54 of her party invitations. She asks her brother Greg to put stamps on them and get them in the morning mail. Greg isn't listening. He forgets the stamps and mails the letters on his way to school.

   _____

   _____

   _____

   _____

3. Manny loves baseball. He never misses a Binghamton Badgers game. Manny has tickets to the Badgers' playoff game on Saturday afternoon. Manny also has a crush on Luisa. Luisa invites Manny to her pool party on Saturday afternoon.

   _____

   _____

   _____

   _____

4. Jackson's mother has a rule—no eating in the living room! Jackson's mother is at work, and Jackson decides to have lunch in the living room and watch television. Jackson puts his bowl of spaghetti and meatballs on the couch and gets up to change the TV channel. Jackson's dog Argus comes running into the room and jumps on the couch.

   _____

   _____

   _____

5. Kelly is deathly afraid of spiders. While riding on a crowded elevator, Kelly feels something tickle her wrist. She looks down and sees a huge spider climbing up her arm.

   _____

   _____

   _____

   _____

You infer when you make assumptions based on the given information.

Directions: *Read each paragraph, then answer the prediction questions and make your revisions. Use the back of the page to predict the outcome of Saturday's race.*

Reid peered through the window of Backstreet Bikes; his blue eyes transfixed on the sleek red racer, which was prominently displayed. If only he could devise a way to buy the racer before Saturday's tournament. Reid knew he'd be victorious if he had the racer; he was the best rider, but he was currently the owner of the worst bike.

1. Without a new bike, predict how Reid will finish in the race. _____

   _____

2. What information supports your predictions? _____

   _____

Mr. Eason, the owner of Backstreet Bikes, walked up behind Reid. "Nice bike," he commented. Reid was jolted out of his little trance. He nodded in agreement, still not looking away from the racer, as if it would disappear if he so much as blinked. "I've seen you ride, boy," continued Mr. Eason. "You're a very talented rider. Bet you could break records on a bike of that caliber." Reid blushed; maybe there was a way he could ride the red racer on Saturday, even if he didn't have the money to buy it.

3. What do you think Reid is planning? _____

   _____

4. Why might Mr. Eason entertain a deal? _____

   _____

5. What statements would lead you to believe that Mr. Eason is a fan of Reid's? _____

   _____

Sir," said Reid, summoning up his nerve. "Sir, I think I have a way that you can sell bikes and I can win." Mr. Eason smiled and rubbed his chin. "If you lend me a bike I'll wear a Backstreet Bikes helmet and jacket in the race. I promise to win and then promote your shop in all my interviews."

6. Will Mr. Eason agree to Reid's offer? Why or why not? _____

   _____

   _____

Name: _____ **Date:** _____

Wanda is a kind person but she dislikes cats ever since a mad cat chased her up a tree in kindergarten. The fire department had to be called to get Wanda down; it was very frightening, not to mention embarrassing! Wanda loves her aunt Trudy, who happens to live with seven feline companions. Aunt Trudy is going to France for ten days. She usually asks her neighbor Freda to watch the kitties when she is away. However, Freda has a broken leg and won't be able to walk for a month. Aunt Trudy asks Wanda for a special favor.

1. What favor does Aunt Trudy ask? _____

2. Do you think Aunt Trudy regrets having to ask this favor of Wanda? Why? _____

_____

3. Will Wanda watch the cats? Why or why not? _____

_____

4. If Wanda were to watch the kitties, do you think she will take good care of them? Why or

why not? _____

_____

Henry needs two more baseball cards—Buster Smith and Dusty Jones—to complete his set of All Star heroes. Henry is obsessed with having the set complete and his mother is becoming concerned. She has forbidden him to buy another card. Henry's mother asks him to make a deposit for her at the bank. She gives Henry $50 in cash and another $75 in signed checks. While walking to the bank, Henry runs into Joey, another card collector. Joey shows Henry Buster Smith and Dusty Jones cards and tells him that they are for sale, if Henry has $50 in cash to pay for them. If not, Joey will offer them to another buyer.

5. What does Henry do? Why? _____

_____

6. What do you think Henry's mother would say if Henry buys the cards with her money?

Why? _____

_____

7. Why might Joey think he has a sure sale? _____

_____

8. What would you do if you were Henry? _____

_____

A table of contents is like a map for a book. It lists all the things you'll read about along the way!

Directions: Refer to the Table of Contents below to answer the following questions.

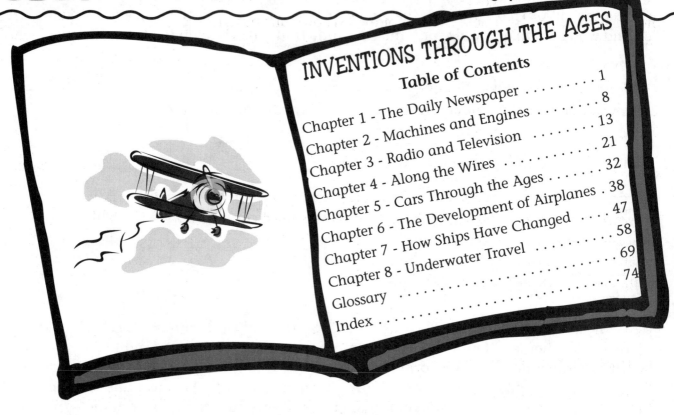

INVENTIONS THROUGH THE AGES
Table of Contents

1. Where would you find information about Henry Ford and the Model T? _____
2. In what chapter might Alexander Graham Bell's inventions be discussed? _____
3 Which chapter contains information about Naval submarines? _____
4. If you were doing a report on the Industrial Revolution, which chapter would you consult first? _____
5. Which chapter is the shortest? _____
6. Where would you find information about sitcoms and transistor radios? _____
7. Where would you probably find information about William Randolph Hearst (newspaper tycoon)? _____
8. Which chapter would discuss the Wright brothers? _____
9. Where can you find selected word definitions? _____
10. What is listed in the index? _____

Write an introduction to the book based on the table of contents on the back of this page.

Name: _____   **Date:** _____

PLANT LIFE DISCOVERED BEYOND EARTH

By Leonard Estrada

Astronauts recently discovered a type of plant growing on the planet Venus. The strangely colored plant was brought back to Earth on Atlantis III, when it returned home from its month-long mission last Friday.

The huge plant resembles a Sago palm; it is hunter green in hue with deep shades of purple and yellow running down the center of each leaf. When broken, the leaves emit a sweet, viscous liquid, that smells very much like coconut milk.

Pictured above is the plant that the Atlantis III crew brought back from Venus.

Scientists are using great caution during the plant's examination process. Protective suits, gloves, and goggles must be worn at all times. It is believed that the plant's juice can cause hallucinations if its liquid is ingested or absorbed through the skin. Only scientists with Level 5 security clearance are permitted to view the plant. It is being housed at an undisclosed military facility until further tests can be completed.

1. Think of another title for the article. _____

2. Who is the author of the article? _____

3. What precautions are taking place? _____

4. What part of the body do goggles protect? _____

5. Why do you think precautions are necessary? _____

6. What are hallucinations? _____

7. What does the word ingest mean? _____

8. What might be an appropriate name for the new plant? _____

9. Why do you think strict security measures are being taken?_____

   _____

10. Who might have use for the plant and why? _____

   _____

Name: _____   **Date:** _____

There are four rules of life.

Speak and act the truth: If you are unable to speak or act the truth, then do not speak or act at all. Lies and harmful actions corrode friendships, harmony, and unity. Always think how your words and deeds will affect others and then decide if the effect will be favorable or unfavorable. Unfavorable is never the correct choice.

_____

_____

Do not judge others: No one is perfect and every story has two sides. If we judge others harshly before we know all of the facts, we sentence that person to emotional prison. The same is true for believing a person to be perfect. In doing so we put him or her on an undeserved pedestal.

_____

_____

Do not judge yourself by what others say: People can make you believe that you are wicked or wonderful. They can hurt your feelings or give you a sense of false security. If you are heavily influenced by others' opinions, you can never be yourself.

_____

_____

Always do your best: Know what you are capable of and do no more and no less. Your capabilities are ever changing, depending on your health, age, and the situation. To do less than your best will cause you to fall short of your potential and leave some of your talents unused.

_____

_____

Name: _____   **Date:** _____

gale

precaution

reputation   indecisive

daunting   maneuver

canvas   postpone

apprehensive

peril

A main idea can be summarized in one sentence.

Anytime you are outdoors, you are at risk for sunburn and possibly skin cancer. Sunburns are your body's way of telling you that it has been exposed to too much direct sunlight. One of the first signs of mild sunburn is the reddening of the skin. The affected area will feel warm and look blotchy-pink. To prevent sunburn, always shield yourself from the sun's powerful rays by wearing protective clothing, sunglasses, hats, and sunscreen with a rating of at least SPF 15.

1. What is the main idea of this paragraph? _____

_____

2. Write two details that support the main idea. _____

_____

_____

_____

Many children and adults drown every year in water-related accidents. Swimming in a pool, lake, or ocean can prove dangerous and even fatal if not done with caution. When in the water, stay safe by following a few simple rules:
• Always swim where a lifeguard is on duty
• Read the signs first—beware of riptides and other natural dangers
• Do not engage in "horseplay"
• Know your limitations and do not exceed them
• Do not swim if you are taking medications that alter your balance or perception

3. What is the main idea of this paragraph? _____

_____

4. Write two details that support the main idea. _____

_____

_____

_____

Name: _____ **Date:** _____

Joe was bored and looking for a solution to the day's tedium. He wandered around the house pondering a way to entertain himself. He spotted his brother's kite—just the distraction he was looking for! However, Joe knew Bob would be mad at him if he borrowed the kite without permission. Joe glanced out the hall window. The trees were blowing in an easterly direction and the sky was bright with white, fluffy clouds and sunshine. Joe knew the kite would soar on a perfectly windy day like this.

Joe went into his brother's room, grabbed the kite, and threw caution to the wind—literally! Joe headed for the park. As Joe unwound the kite's long string, he heard a familiar voice. "Hey there, little brother," growled Bob. "What do you think you're doing?"

1. What is the main idea of the story? _____

_____

2. Finish the story. _____

_____

_____

"Working animals deserve rights just like working humans!" shouted Eloise into a microphone as she stood atop the auditorium stage. The crowd burst into applause. "They should be given set working hours and liberal vacations. Animals should even be compensated for overtime, and female animals deserve maternity leave!" Again, the crowd cheered.

It was Eloise's mission in life to defend the rights of animals. She had been doing so ever since her parents took her on a carriage ride through Central Park. It was July 1, 1992, Eloise's tenth birthday. The weather was extremely hot and the horse was having difficulty breathing. Instead of returning the languid animal to the stables, the carriage driver angrily whipped the pathetic beast. Eloise was appalled! She jumped out of her seat and took matters into her own hands.

3. What is the main idea of the story? _____

_____

4. What you think happened next? Finish the story. _____

_____

_____

_____

Name: _____   **Date:** _____

More people die in fires than in hurricanes, earthquakes, floods and all other natural disasters combined! Fires are very dangerous. Every year children start more than 100,000 fires. These fires account for thousands of deaths and millions of dollars in property damage. Dangerous fires can be prevented in many ways; the first is to take fire seriously and the second is to prepare in the event of a fire.

1. What is the main idea? _____

    a. Fires are dangerous.

    b. Children are dangerous.

    c. Fires are worse than earthquakes.

No music collection is complete without a Beatles CD. That is because the Beatles are the most influential band of the 20th century. Back in the '60s the Beatles routinely topped the charts with hits like "Paperback Writer" and "Yellow Submarine." They sold millions of records, appeared in movies and on television, and have had dozens of books written about them. Even today, many Beatles songs receive regular radio airplay—they are considered classic hits.

2. What is the main idea? _____

    a. CDs are better than records.

    b. No music collection is complete without a Beatles CD.

    c. The Beatles were popular only in the '60s.

If it could be mass-produced, spider silk would be a hot commodity. Spider silk is an amazing fiber. Spider silk is stronger than steel and has more stretch than rubber. So why don't we see spider silk clothing that never wears out and thin spider silk ropes that can hold back a Mack truck? The problem is that spiders do not cohabitate well with members of their species. They do not have the friendly manners of silkworms! Spiders fight when in groups and eat one another. Therefore, it is impossible for spiders to make enough silk on their own to manufacture human products.

3. What is the main idea? _____

    a. Spider silk clothing will replace wool.

    b. Spiders are natural-born fighters.

    c. Spider silk is an amazing fiber.

 Name: _____   **Date:** _____

Conclusions tell how the story ends based on the given facts.

Directions: *Read the story then draw your own conclusions by answering the questions below. Support all of your conclusions with information from the story.*

Jennifer was reading a novel. Ronnie began telling another of his made-up stories out loud. "Oh, chill Ronnie," smiled Jennifer, finally putting down her novel. "I do listen to you, sometimes. But we've been cooped up in this musty, drafty cabin for two days and I'm getting a little exhausted by your non-ending stories. They aren't only ridiculous, but they are boring." She saw by Ronnie's expression that his feelings were deeply hurt. Jennifer tried to ease the sting of her words. "I'm sorry. It's just that I thought we were going to have a fun ski vacation. Who knew an avalanche was going to close the slopes and block all the exit roads for this long? I'm as bored as you are. I just happen to be better at entertaining myself than you are."

Ronnie was still looking dejected. "How am I ever going to be a famous author if I can't even get my sister to listen to my stories?"

"I have an idea," Jennifer offered. "Why don't you write me a story, Ronnie? That way you can gather your thoughts before you express them, and while you are writing I can have the quiet I'm craving." Ronnie agreed.

1. What time of the year does the story take place? How do you know? _____

2. Describe the place where Jennifer and Ronnie are staying. _____

3. Does Jennifer like to read? How do you know? _____

4. If given the chance, do you think Jennifer would leave the cabin? Why? _____
_____

5. How is Ronnie dealing with his boredom? _____

6. What is Ronnie's future ambition? _____

7. Do you think Ronnie is quiet while he writes? Why or why not? _____
_____

8. If given the opportunity, do you think Ronnie and Jennifer would leave the cabin and go home? Why or why not? _____

9. How do you think their vacation will end? _____

10. Think of three adjectives that describe the characters:

    Ronnie: _____

    Jennifer: _____

Name: _____   **Date:** _____

Reading Comprehension • Saddleback Publishing, Inc. ©2002   61   3 Watson, Irvine, CA 92618•Phone (888)SDL-BACK•www.sdlback.com

_____ 1. The Golden State is really beautiful. I am looking out of my hotel window at the largest suspension bridge in the world. Tomorrow I will travel south to stargaze at all the famous people. Then I will go south of the border to visit a Spanish-speaking country.

_____ 2. Today I went for a swim in a great salt lake. The Sundance Film Festival is being held nearby. In the winter this state has many great places to ski and snowboard, such as Park City and Deer Valley.

_____ 3. Aloha! As I arrived in this island paradise, I was presented with a beautiful flower lei. These islands are warm and humid, and have many beautiful beaches with large waves perfect for surfing. This state is the most recent addition to the United States of America.

_____ 4. Howdy, partner! I am visiting the Lone Star State. Everything is bigger here. I've seen many cowboys and large herds of cattle, as well as lots of oil wells. The men all wear big hats and everyone loves to squaredance and listen to country music.

_____ 5. Here I am in America's last great wilderness. This is a good state to visit in the summer because the days last forever, and there's a lot to see and do. Tomorrow we are going to pan for gold and then go salmon fishing in the river. During the winter everyone stays indoors a lot because it is very cold and the days are extremely short.

_____ 6. I am in a taxi in the Big Apple on my way to see some Broadway shows. Most people use the subway to travel in this city. This city was originally called New Amsterdam, but now it has the same name as the state where it's located.

_____ 7. Today I am relaxing on a beautiful white sand beach, while enjoying a large glass of fresh orange juice, both of which this state is famous for. Tomorrow I will explore the Everglades, and then go to visit the oldest city in America.

_____ 8. Greetings from a New England state that shares borders with Massachusetts, Maine, and Vermont. The leaves, wearing their fall colors of red and gold, are beautiful here. While visiting the state capital, Concord, I learned that the state motto is Live Free or Die.

_____ 9. Wow! Mt. Rushmore is really impressive. Some of the Indian tribes that live here include the Lakota, Dakota, and Nakota, which make up the Sioux Indian Nation.

_____ 10. Here I am on a riverboat, heading toward the Gulf of Mexico. This mighty river has the same name as the state it borders. The fishing is great. Wish you were here.

a. Utah	b. North Dakota	c. Mississippi	d. California	e. Maine
f. Florida	g. Hawaii	h. Texas	i. Alaska	j. New York

Name: _____   **Date:** _____

Paying attention to the surrounding words in a sentence can assist you in learning new vocabulary words.

Directions: *Read the sentence. Then write the meaning of the word used in the sentence. Use a dictionary to assist you.*

1. Their adversaries had already staked out their territory and were prepared for battle.

   "Adversaries" means _____

2. Without the general's sanction to charge, the soldiers were forced to wait.

   "Sanction" means _____

3. The soldiers alleged the enemy was shooting at them as they tried to cross the river.

   "Alleged" means _____

4. The enemy scout vanished into the woods before the troops spotted him.

   "Vanished" means _____

5. A condolence telegram was sent to the family of the missing soldier.

   "Condolence" means _____

6. A shrine now stands in honor of the brave men who fought in the battle.

   "Shrine" means _____

7. When people pass by the dedication, many emotions are stirred within their hearts.

   "Stirred" means _____

8. Sometimes private endowments are made to help with the monument's upkeep.

   "Endowment" means _____

9. A commission meets to decide on budgeting.

   "Commission" means _____

10. The government made an allocation of millions of dollars to repair the roads.

    "Allocation" means _____

11. These adventurous men are willing to fight to protect their country.

    "Adventurous" means _____

Name: _____   **Date:** _____

Human bones are <u>composed</u> of two important minerals: calcium and phosphorus. With the help of these minerals, your body will develop and <u>maintain</u> a strong skeletal structure. It is important to <u>consume</u> foods that are rich in these minerals. <u>Dairy</u> products, such as milk, cheese, yogurt, and ice cream, are excellent sources.

<u>Osteoporosis</u> is a <u>degenerative</u> bone disease, resulting in a loss of bone tissue, that usually affects <u>mature</u> women. But the disease can be prevented. Our bodies require a <u>nutritious</u> diet and regular exercise. Young women should make a conscious effort to take a calcium supplement and <u>partake</u> in a regular exercise program.

Doctors advise women to exercise at least three times a week. Running, jogging, jumping rope, aerobics, dancing, cycling, skating, and swimming are all great <u>aerobic</u> activities. It is also important to include bone-strengthening <u>anaerobic</u> activities in your exercise routine. This combination of exercises will help build up your strength, muscle power, and <u>flexibility</u>. Proper diet and exercise can lessen your chances of developing osteoporosis.

1. composed _____

2. maintain _____

3. consume _____

4. dairy _____

5. osteoporosis _____

6. degenerative _____

7. mature _____

8. nutritious _____

9. partake _____

10. aerobic _____

11. anaerobic _____

12. flexibility _____

Name: _____   **Date:** _____

> **Previewing is viewing all of the elements first, then seeing the complete picture.**

Directions: *For each board game description below, answer the two questions in complete sentences.*

This game comes in a red box and has pictures of running chickens on it. Inside the box is a timer, a CD for music, a big picture with a racetrack on it, scorecards, pencils and, of course, chickens.

1. Without reading the directions, how do you think you would play this game?

_____

_____

_____

2. What would be a good name for this game? _____

The pieces for this game contain three boxes of clay, a spinner that picks a category, a card deck describing categories such as animals, sports, places, food, and household objects, four pegs, and a note pad scoring sheet.

1. Without any the directions how do you think this game is played? _____

_____

_____

_____

2. What would be a fitting name for this game? _____

This game comes in a soft, felt black bag covered in stars. Inside the bag are a small red ball, some yarn, a bell and a 4-foot mat with colored squares on it.

1. How do you think this game is played? _____

_____

_____

_____

2. What would be a neat name for this game? _____

Name: _____ **Date:** _____

Supporting sentences always back up what the topic sentence says.

Directions: *Supporting sentences give validity to the main idea or topic sentence. Read the topic sentences below and then put a check (✓) next to the sentences that support it.*

A. Roman coins offer a unique view into ancient Roman life.

_____ 1. Roman coins were used by almost everyone on a daily basis, from the emperor down to the merchant.

_____ 2. American coins are made out of various durable metals.

_____ 3. Coins tell us much about what was important to the Roman people, how they celebrated holidays and religious occasions, and how the emperors wanted to be viewed by their subjects.

_____ 4. The quarter is larger than the penny, but smaller than a silver dollar.

_____ 5. Coins give us excellent portraits of the emperors, their wives and children, and famous buildings that have long ago crumbled into ruin.

B. Roman gladiators were recruited from many different places.

_____ 1. Captured soldiers were a popular source because soldiers were already trained to fight.

_____ 2. The movie *Gladiator* is a fictional movie, based on fact.

_____ 3. Free citizens could and did become gladiators. It was a popular choice for the poor. Gladiators got three square meals a day, decent medical care, and if they were good, survived to freedom. They also had the opportunity to win money.

_____ 4. Women fought as gladiators.

_____ 5. Regardless of where they came from, gladiators all had to agree to the same five conditions: a) being branded; b) being chained; c) being killed by an iron weapon; d) to pay with their blood for the food and drink they received; and e) to suffer pain even if they did not wish to.

_____ 6. Masters sold their undisciplined and difficult slaves to gladiator schools.

Dear Gabby,
My life is in constant danger thanks to Broxton Bronco, the school bully. He follows me home from school and yells rude things at me and even threatens to hurt me if I tell. He steals my lunch money regularly and insists that I let him copy my homework. I have tried talking to my teacher about this, but she says that I shouldn't be a tattletale and that I should just ignore Broxton. Please help me!

Signed,
Petrified Pete

Problem: _____
_____
_____
_____

Solution: _____
_____
_____
_____
_____

Dear Gabby,
There's this boy at my school who is always very nice to me. He always shared snacks with me in the cafeteria and even invited me to watch him play baseball once! Last week we were talking and our math teacher told him to stop flirting with me out loud in front of the whole class. Everyone laughed. Now he doesn't talk to me anymore. He says that he doesn't even like me and that he was just trying to be nice. I am very upset. Did he really like me or was he just trying to be nice?

Signed,
Sad Sandy

Problem: _____
_____
_____
_____

Solution: _____
_____
_____
_____
_____

Dear Gabby,
I really liked a girl at my school. I decided to ask her out, and now she has changed! She follows me everywhere and gets jealous when I talk to my friends. Every night she calls me about ten times and even leaves messages for me when I am trying to do my homework. My parents are getting mad and I don't know what to do. I told her to stop being so pesky but she said she just likes me a lot.

Signed,
Troubled Ted

Problem: _____
_____
_____
_____

Solution: _____
_____
_____
_____
_____

Kenny had been saving his allowance and gift money for the past seven months. He even took on a part-time job after school—walking Mrs. Dripper's hyperactive dog Droplet. Kenny's goal was to save enough money to buy a Phase VII Surf Dude Windsurfer, just like the one Rex Riggs rode in the Hawaiian championship. Kenny knew the windsurfer would be expensive and he was glad his dad promised to match every dollar Kenny had saved and earned.

The windsurfer was scheduled for release on June 30th. On the night of the 29th, Kenny counted his cash. He had $347; with his dad's matching donation, Kenny had a total of $694.

Kenny woke up the next morning very excited. His dad was already awake and waiting to drive Kenny to the surf shop. There was a crowd of kids huddled around the shop entrance. Kenny could see the Phase VII Surfer Dude prominently displayed in the window. His heart raced as he strained to see the price, which was being blocked by a kid with a huge head. Then he caught a glimpse. "Only $899" read the sign. Kenny could feel tears welling up in his eyes and a lump forming in his throat.

What's Kenny's problem? _____

_____

How do you think he will solve the problem? Why? _____

_____

_____

NOW IT'S YOUR TURN…

What problem did you have to overcome?_____

_____

How did you solve it? _____

_____

_____

_____

Grids, labels, charts, and diagrams offer quick ways of organizing and reading information.

Directions: *Read the grid below. Then answer the questions.*

Pine Knot Elementary School had a magazine subscription drive. See how many subscriptions each classroom sold. The winning class was rewarded with an ice cream party. Every classroom that participated received a new book for their classroom library.

MAGAZINE SUBSCRIPTIONS	
Room 2	.10 subscriptions
Room 4	.17 subscriptions
Room 6	.8 subscriptions
Room 8	.11 subscriptions
Room 10	.32 subscriptions
Room 12	.25 subscriptions
Room 14	.19 subscriptions
Room 16	.15 subscriptions
Room 18	.19 subscriptions
Room 20	.22 subscriptions
Room 22	.28 subscriptions
Pine Knot School	.206 subscriptions

1. How many subscriptions did Room 12 sell? _____

2. Which classroom had the ice cream party? _____

3. Which classroom sold the least amount of subscriptions? _____

4. Which classrooms sold the same amount of subscriptions? _____

5. Which classroom sold the second most subscriptions? _____

6. How many classrooms participated in all? _____

7. How many subscriptions did Pine Knot Elementary School sell in all? _____

8. Which classroom sold 17 subscriptions? _____

Name: _____   **Date:** _____

One cold and rainy afternoon, Connor's mom made him a warm, delicious lunch. He ate two bowls of tomato soup and five crackers. Below are the labels from the can of tomato soup and the box of crackers. How nourishing was Connor's lunch?

TOMATO SOUP	
NUTRITION FACTS	
Serving Size	1 bowl
Servings per can	2
Calories	80
Total Fat	0 grams
Cholesterol	0 mg
Sodium	710 mg
Total Carbohydrates	19g
Fiber	1 gram
Protein	2 grams

CRACKERS	
NUTRITION FACTS	
Serving Size	5 crackers
Servings per box	7
Calories	70
Total Fat	1.5 grams
Cholesterol	0 mg
Sodium	100 mg
Total Carbohydrates	13g
Fiber	less than 1 gram
Protein	2 grams

1. How many servings of soup did Connor eat for lunch? _____

2. How much sodium is in five crackers? _____

3. What was the total amount of fat in the tomato soup? _____

4. How do you know that Connor finished the entire can of soup? _____

_____

5. How much fiber was in the soup? _____

6. How many grams of protein were in the crackers? _____

7. How much cholesterol did Connor consume by eating the soup and crackers?

_____

8. How many calories did Connor have at lunch? _____

9. How many carbohydrates were in the can of tomato soup? _____

10. What other food group do you think Connor should have added to the meal

to make it more complete? _____

Directions: *Examine the frog life cycle diagram. Interpret and explain its meaning on the lines below. Use the out-of-order phrases below as your guide.*

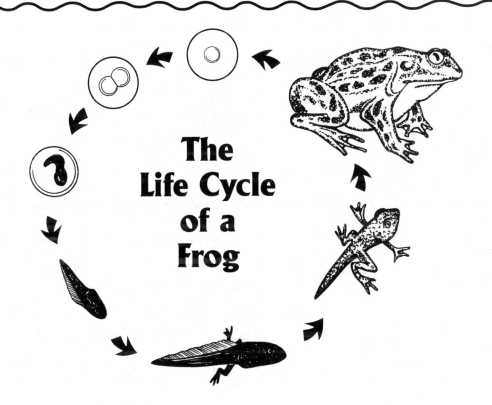

The Life Cycle of a Frog

Not yet a frog.	An embryo is formed.	The tadpole begins to change.
It's a tadpole.	The egg is laid.	It's a frog! The cells split.

_____

_____

_____

_____

_____

_____

_____

_____

_____

Name: _____ **Date:** _____

Lions

Live in family groups called prides.

Can still be found in the wild in Africa.

Male lions grow a mane around the age of 2.

Females do most of the hunting for the pride.

A lion's roar can be heard up to five miles away.

Lions & Tigers

They are found in Asia.

Their fur acts as camouflage.

They are threatened by habitat loss and poaching.

They are members of the *Panthera* family.

Tigers

Tigers like the water.

Tigers can live in a variety of habitats, from the snows of Siberia to the jungles of Sumatra.

They are solitary animals.

Tigers' stripes make them hard to see in the jungle.

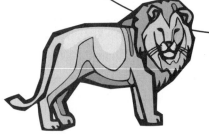

1. Which is a solitary animal?
_____

2. Which is found in Asia?
_____

3. Which lives in a pride?
_____

4. Which likes water?
_____

5. Which is a member of the *Panthera* family?
_____

6. Which grows a mane?
_____

7. Which females do most of the hunting?
_____

8. Which can be found in Siberia?
_____

9. Which is threatened by habitat loss?
_____

10. Which has stripes to give it camouflage?
_____

Name: _____   **Date:** _____

Answer the questions about these cartoon characters below with the information found in the matrix.

Burt Bunny	Likes to eat carrots.	Lives in a burrow.	Has an English accent.	First came on television in 1979.
Emit Crumm	Is always trying to pollute Burt Bunny's forest.	Has never taken a bath and is proud of it.	Speaks with food in his mouth.	Was introduced on the Burt Bunny show in 1980.
Dopey Dog	Has long ears that he trips over.	Has a sidekick named Flea.	Can speak six languages, including cat.	Was voted "Best Cartoon Character" in 1995.
Scruffy	Will do almost anything for a Dooby snack.	Has a sidekick named Dooby.	Needs a haircut.	First aired in 1999.
Lop & Larry	Are connected at the tail.	Lop is a gerbil and Larry is a rat.	Were created by Dr. Vic Vet in a science experiment.	Have been on television since 1988.

1. Who probably smells bad? _____

2. Who has a sidekick named Flea? _____

3. Which characters were created by Dr. Vic Vet? _____

4. Which character has been on television
   the shortest amount of time? _____

5. Which two characters have long ears? _____

6. Who is Dooby? _____

7. Who lives in a hole in the ground? _____

8. Who has been on television 11 years longer than Scruffy? _____

9. Who made his television debut in 1980? _____

10. Who speaks cat? _____

United States	Declared its independence in 1776.	Is composed of 50 states.	Is governed by a president.
England	Once ruled the United States.	Also called Great Britain.	Still recognizes a monarchy.
China	Is the most populated country.	Is the only place where pandas still roam free.	Is located on the continent of Asia.
Australia	Is a country and a continent.	Is the native home to Aborigines.	Has a kangaroo on its flag.
Spain	Is located on the continent of Europe.	Native language is Spanish.	Funded Christopher Columbus' voyage.

1. _____ once ruled the United States.

2. Pandas still roam free in the mountains of _____.

3. _____ is a country and a continent.

4. The United States is composed of _____ states.

5. Columbus received his three ships from the king and queen of _____.

6. Aborigines are native to this country _____.

7. Spanish is the native language of _____.

8. _____ is the most populated country in the world.

9. _____ is also called Great Britain.

10. The United States declared its independence in _____.

Directions: *Read the sentences below and decide whether they are fact or opinion. You may wish to use an encyclopedia for help.*

1. The Earth's solar system contains nine planets.

2. Mercury is closest to the sun.

3. Mars is not the coldest planet.

4. Pluto is a useless planet.

5. I think space creatures are living on Venus.

6. Saturn has 28 moons.

7. Uranus is the planet with the weirdest name.

8. Neptune is a big ball of gas with a metal core.

9. Everyone likes movies about outer space.

10. The sun is more than 100 times larger than the Earth.

11. Everyone should get a chance to travel into space.

12. Mars is also called the red planet.

13. A day on Venus is 243 Earth days long.

14. In Roman mythology, Saturn is the god of agriculture.

15. I think kids should have to learn about the planets.

16. The Earth's Moon was first visited by the Soviet spacecraft Luna 2 in 1959.

17. One of the principal objectives of the Voyager 1 mission was the study of Titan, which is one of Saturn's satellites.

18. The U.S. government spends too much tax money on space exploration.

19. A tax should be added for all airline flights to fund space travel for kids.

20. Neptune has been visited by only one spacecraft, Voyager 2, on Aug. 25, 1989.

Name: _____   **Date:** _____

Old Joe Johnson lives next door to me. Joe is ancient—I'd guess about 300 years old. When Joe was born, the Revolutionary War was just beginning, and a kid's idea of fun was chasing squirrels and eating tree bark. Joe reads 50 books a day, and I'm not talking little books, either. I mean huge tomes, even longer than the telephone directory! Joe gets most of his books from the library and garage sales.

Last weekend I went to a garage sale with Joe. These people had so much stuff in their garage that a worm couldn't even fit in to look around. And the place smelled like dusty socks were kept there for 100 years. I thought my nose hairs were going to disintegrate. Joe didn't seem to notice the smell or the mess. All he could see were the stacks of books—$5 a bagful. They had a bunch of crinkled old grocery bags and people were filling them full of musty books. Joe must have gotten 1,000 books in his bag! Then he asked me to carry it. The darn thing was heavier than an elephant in armor. Joe was all worried that I'd dump the bag, but I didn't. I carried them over the mountains and through the woods back to Joe's house. Joe was very tired when we got there. He sat down on his porch and was deep into a nap before I could say, "How about some lemonade?" I figured, what the heck, and pulled up a chair. Before I knew it, I was lost in my own world of shuteye! Garage sales sure are tiring.

Exaggeration: _____

_____

_____

_____

_____

_____

_____

_____

_____

_____

_____

_____

_____

Rudd Flynn is thirteen years old. Rudd lives in the tiny village of Trundle. Rudd is quite unlike other children his age, because Rudd is a junior-apprentice sorcerer, first class. A junior-apprentice sorcerer, first class has been through two years of intense magical training and has the knowledge and the authorization to cast spells, tame monsters, and alter the weather. Sorcerers seem to stumble upon adventures the way mortals stumble upon uneven stones and bricks in the road. This was the case recently when Rudd found himself face-to-face with a gerbilgoff.

Gerbilgoffs, for those of you who are not familiar, are fanciful creatures that resemble gerbils except for the fact that they grow to be over 7' tall and are fierce aggressors if their nests are disturbed. Gerbilgoffs fear lightning. So when Rudd accidentally disturbed a nest of grunts (the term used to describe baby gerbilgoffs) and their mother lunged in ominous retaliation, Rudd was left with no other option but to produce a bolt of lightning from the tip of his wand. It scared the gerbilgoff, but it also triggered the biggest electrical storm Trundle has seen in decades.

Electrical storms can be quite dangerous. Rudd had to ensure the safety of the townspeople so he materialized warning signs and magically hung them in every shop window. They read: During an electrical storm, please—

- Get inside a building, if possible.
- Keep away from windows and open doors.
- Don't use electrical appliances or the telephone. Lightning can follow the wires into your home.
- Stay out of the shower or bathtub. Lightning can travel through the pipes, too.
- Avoid trees, poles and other tall objects.
- Also avoid large metal objects. These things are targets for lightning.
- Go to low ground and crouch down low if you're caught outdoors.
- If you're in the water, get out as quickly as possible.

That way everyone in Trundle was safe from the storm.

Factual: _____

_____

_____

_____

Fantasy: _____

_____

_____

_____

Name: _____ **Date:** _____

Directions: *Read the story. Rewrite the story on the lines below; omit the trivial and redundant information.*

Marshall examined the scene of the theft. He looked around the place where the chocolate bunny had disappeared. Sticky footprints led toward the stairs. They weren't human prints. Marshall only likes sour candy balls. He never eats chocolate because it gives him a rash.

"I think it was a ghost!" declared Marshall's sister Missy, the owner of the missing chocolate. "I didn't hear them come in or out, and I was here the entire time. I was listening but I didn't hear a thing."

Marshall wrote that fact down in his notebook. He wrote in pen. He likes to write in pen better than in pencil. It makes him feel more grown up.

Just as Marshall was finishing his notes, Buttercup, Missy's cat, walked into the room. Her face and paws were brown. "Look," said Missy, "Buttercup has been playing in the mud."

Name: _____ Date: _____

Monster parties are fun to host, even if it's not Halloween.

You can have lots of enjoyment hosting a monster party.

The word Halloween rhymes with the color green.

The coolest thing about monster parties is the monster food.

You can make delicious monster guts by mixing cooked spaghetti with red Jell-O®.

Disgusting fingers are easy to make, too—they're hotdogs sliced in half and doused in ketchup.

I always show scary movies at my monster parties; my favorite is *Ghastly Ghouls from the Grave.*

If you play the video in reverse, it's funny and scary!

Our VCR is brand new.

Write your invitations in red pen, because it looks like blood!

My sister lost her first tooth, yesterday.

_____

_____

_____

_____

_____

_____

_____

_____

_____

_____

_____

_____

Name: _____   **Date:** _____

Keep things straight—use your logic to sequence things you read.

Directions: Rewrite the sentences in the correct sequence on the lines below. (There can be variations in the order of the sentences.)

- Bud and his wife wanted very badly to have a child, but they could not have a child of their own.
- The children looked very sad, even though they were smiling.
- Betty cried when she saw the pictures in the article.
- One little girl in particular left an impression on Bud.
- Bud and Betty decided to adopt the orphan child.
- The Buttons family lived happily ever after.
- Bud's heartstrings were instantly pulled tight.
- The picture showed many orphan boys and girls in need of a home.
- Her large eyes and cherub smile reminded Bud of his dear mother, Bea.
- The Buttons became a family of three with their daughter named Brie.
- Bud and his wife called the adoption agency the next morning.
- One evening Bud was looking through a magazine and saw a picture that made him think.
- Once upon a time there was a couple named Bud and Betty Buttons.
- Bud showed the article to his wife, Betty.

_____

_____

_____

_____

_____

_____

_____

_____

_____

_____

_____

_____

Name: _____   **Date:** _____

Snuggles and Muggles wondered if there were other rabbits in the world. Muggles ate so much, he could barely hop. The rabbits lived in a hutch owned by the Smith family. Snuggles and Muggles decided to investigate the yard. The garden was full of exotic vegetables, many they'd never before tasted. From then on, Snuggles and Muggles were content to stay at home in their safe hutch. They were so busy tasting everything, they didn't notice there was a large, yellow cat crouched behind a tomato bush. "Hop!" yelled Muggles, and the two bunnies didn't stop hopping until they were safely back in their hutch. Then they hopped over to the garden on the other side of the Smith's fence. Once upon a time, there were two rabbits. Snuggles hopped out first and landed in a pile of leaves, followed by Muggles. First, they encountered many delicious flowers. One morning Snuggles noticed that the hutch door was unlocked. Suddenly the creature pounced (leaped toward them). The hutch provided warmth and shelter for Snuggles and Muggles, and their owners fed them every day, but something was lacking.

_____

_____

_____

_____

_____

_____

_____

_____

_____

_____

_____

_____

_____

Name: _____ **Date:** _____

Genre is a book's category or type. A book's genre has a certain style or form, such as science fiction.

Directions: Read the book jacket titles and summaries. Determine each book's genre. Refer to the selections below.

Biography	Fiction	Autobiography	Mystery/Suspense
Self-Help	Travel	Non-Fiction	Science Fiction

Jelly Fish and the Missing Whale

Jelly is no fish; she's a detective, hired to find the Museum of Natural History's missing whale. Is it being kept in a flight hanger at JFK? Jelly has clues that are telling.

1. Genre: _____

Alien Aardvarks

Hosing-up humans with their long sucking noses! Will the Earth be saved from these menacing creatures? The Federation has called on its best space warriors, but is there enough time? Hold on to your seat, this is truly a page turner!

2. Genre: _____

Travels with Trevor

I've seen London; I've seen France. Rode a camel in my khaki. If you want the skinny on exotic vacation locations, this is your book.

3. Genre: _____

MI VIDA LOCA

This is my insane life, written by me, in my own words.

4. Genre: _____

Name: _____   Date: _____

Biography	Fiction	Autobiography	Mystery/Suspense
Self-Help	Travel	Non-Fiction	Science Fiction

The Life and Times of Abraham Lincoln

A refreshingly new look at the man who was both a president and a statesman.

1. Genre: _____

Nail Biter's Relief

Tired of wearing gloves? End that nasty nail-biting habit forever in 10 easy steps. Let this former finger muncher show you how it's done, once and for all.

2. Genre: _____

Catso and Ratso Return Again

Part 5 in the exciting series adventures of Catso and Ratso, superhero crime-fighting critters. This daring duo does more in a day than dabble in danger. They dig it up!

3. Genre: _____

The Battle of Little Big Horn

What really happened on that fateful day? Was Custer to blame for his own demise? This book contains never-before-seen photographs, maps, and illustrations.

4. Genre: _____

Name: _____ **Date:** _____

Directions: *Read the passage. Then write the topic sentences in each paragraph on the lines below.*

A. Nocturnal animals are very different than most animals you commonly see during your waking hours. Unlike dogs and horses, nocturnal animals do most of their playing, hunting, caring for their young, and exploring in the dark of night. When you are asleep, nocturnal animals are active. In the morning, when you awaken, these animals are going off to burrows and nests to sleep.

B. Nocturnal animals have special adaptations to help them thrive in the dark. Owls have large eyes that can see well on a moonless night. Foxes have a great sense of smell that enables them to locate prey in very little light. Mice, gerbils, and other rodents have long whiskers to guide them safely through the woods at night. Hyenas have large ears that they use to hear sounds and locate prey in the dark, and bats use a form of radar to maneuver through the darkness.

C. Diurnal animals are the opposite of nocturnal animals. Diurnal animals are active during the day and need sunshine to thrive and survive. Diurnal animals tend to have smaller eyes and ears than nocturnal animals because light guides their way. It's possible that a nocturnal and diurnal animal living in the same forest might never encounter one another. You can say one works the night shift while the other works during the day.

A. _____

_____

_____

B. _____

_____

_____

C. _____

_____

_____

Name: _____   **Date:** _____

The common green iguana, scientifically known as *Iguana iguana*, is a reptile pet imported from South or Central America or raised in captivity. Iguanas are the most popular lizard for people to have as pets. Unfortunately, they tend to be a pet bought on impulse. Consequently, owners often do not understand the needs of their pet. One factor people forget about iguanas is that they grow continuously. In the wild, iguanas live 10 to 15 years and can grow as large as 7 feet. Reptiles in captivity can live up to 20 years if cared for properly.

Each reptile has requirements for moisture, temperature, hibernation, and diet. Owning any reptile is going to require work. You can't just buy it, throw it in a cage, and think it's fine. Do research about your potential pet and find out the requirements. You should get a cage that is at least two times the length, from nose to tail, of the reptile. Plus you will want to have room for it to move up and down so you'll need to provide branches for it to climb on. Iguanas are herbivores. Up to 90 percent of an iguana's diet should consist of dark leafy green vegetables.

Iguanas are diurnal. In their native environment, iguanas rest at night and begin the hunt for tender shoots, flowers, and soft fruits after basking in the sun for a few hours in the morning. After eating, they bask in the sun again to stay warm enough to digest food. Be sure to provide your iguana with a source of ultraviolet light and the appropriate amount of heat. Keep a thermometer available to monitor the air temperature.

Iguanas are prey species. So a great part of the day is spent keeping a lookout for predators. Initially, you will be the predator it is protecting itself from. Socializing your iguana is a time-consuming process, but necessary. Many people end up getting rid of their iguana when it expresses its natural behavior of aggressiveness toward the predator—humans. However, with time and socialization with you, your iguana will relax and be a happy, safe pet.

Name: _____   Date: _____

A. Kites have been around for more than two thousand years and have had many uses besides recreation. Kites are believed to have been invented in China or Korea about 200 B.C. One of the earliest kite stories is about a famous Chinese general, Han Hsin. Around 200 B.C. Hsin was the commander of a rebel army on a mission to overthrow an evil emperor. Han ordered his men to build a kite and to fly it over the Emperor's palace. When the kite was over the palace, the string was marked. Later Han measured the length and determined how long a tunnel should be dug to bring the rebel army inside the walls of the palace. His plan was successful and the malevolent Emperor was eventually overthrown.

_____

_____

_____

B. Millions of different kinds of plants and animals live on Earth. Rainforests are home to more than half of those species. Rainforests are an important habitat. Millions of forest-dwelling people around the world live in or depend on rainforests. They have learned how to live in ways that don't harm the forests. Many of the world's important food crops, medicines and animals come from rainforest species. The Earth's weather is affected by rainforests. When trees are cut down and burnt or left to decompose. they release carbon dioxide into the air, which causes global warming.

_____

_____

_____

C. Boxing Day is a holiday celebrated in Britain, Australia, New Zealand, and Canada. It falls on December 26. The public observance of Boxing Day takes place on the following Monday if December 26 falls on a Saturday or Sunday. The traditional celebration of Boxing Day included giving money and other gifts to charitable institutions, needy individuals, and people in service jobs. The holiday may date from the Middle Ages (A.D. 400s–1500s), but the exact origin is unknown. It may have begun with the lords and ladies of England, who presented Christmas gifts in boxes to their servants on December 26.

_____

_____

_____

Name: _____   **Date:** _____

St. Augustine is the oldest permanent European settlement on the North American continent. It was founded forty-two years before the English colony at Jamestown, Virginia, and fifty-five years before the Pilgrims landed on Plymouth Rock in Massachusetts.

St. Augustine is the oldest city in America. Spanish explorer and treasure hunter Don Juan Ponce de Leon first sighted the mainland of North America on Easter, March 27, 1513. He claimed the land for Spain and named it La Florida, meaning "Land of Flowers." Between 1513 and 1563 the government of Spain launched six expeditions to settle Florida, but all failed. The French succeeded in establishing a fort and colony on the St. Johns River in 1564 and, in doing so, threatened Spain's treasure fleets that sailed along Florida's shoreline returning to Spain. As a result of this infiltration into Florida, King Phillip II named Don Pedro Menendez de Aviles, Spain's most experienced admiral, as governor of Florida, instructing him to explore and to colonize the rich territory. Menendez was also instructed to drive out any pirates or settlers from other countries.

Menendez skillfully fulfilled his king's wishes. When Menendez arrived off the coast of Florida it was August 28, 1565, the Feast Day of St. Augustine. Eleven days later, he and his 600 soldiers and settlers came ashore at the site of the Timucuan Indian village of Seloy with Spanish flags flying and trumpets sounding. He quickly fortified the tiny village and named it St. Augustine. Making the most of brilliant military maneuvers, Menendez destroyed the French garrison on the St. Johns River and, with the help of a tropical hurricane, also defeated the French fleet. With the coast of Florida firmly in Spanish hands, he set to work building the town, establishing missions, converting the Indians to his church, and exploring the lush land.

Fascinating Facts:

_____

_____

_____

_____

_____

_____

_____

_____

Look for the main idea and supporting details as you read the information below. Write the main idea and phrases to describe the supporting facts on the spaces provided.

At the end of the Civil War, the defeated South was a ruined land. The physical destruction caused by Union troops was enormous, and the old social and economic order founded on slavery had collapsed completely, with nothing to replace it. Carpetbaggers saw this as an opportunity to prosper. The word carpetbagger was used in the South after the Civil War to describe Northerners who went to the South during reconstruction to seek their fortune. Although regarded as temporary residents of the South because of the carpetbags in which they carried their possessions (hence the name carpetbaggers), most of these opportunists intended to settle in the South and take advantage of business opportunities there. Former slaves were more trusting of Northerners than former slave owners and tended to vote for the outsiders. With the support of the black vote, the carpetbaggers played an important role in the Republican state governments. The corrupt activities of some carpetbaggers made the term carpetbagger one and the same with any stranger who interferes in a town's political affairs for personal benefit.

Main Idea: _____

_____

Supporting Details: _____

_____

_____

_____

_____

_____

_____

_____

_____

_____

1. Mature trees are an important part of nature.

_____

_____

_____

2. No two people are exactly alike.

_____

_____

_____

3. A good book can take you wonderful places.

_____

_____

_____

4. Television has an influence on the way people think.

_____

_____

_____

Take it from me, pal. Look for things that are the same and different when you compare and contrast things.

Directions: Carefully observe these pictures and read the information below. Note the similarities and differences between these two sports on the lines below.

Baseball vs. Golf

Baseball is a team sport. The object of the game is to hit the ball so the other team can't catch it and run around the bases until you reach home. There are nine innings in a baseball game, unless there is a tie, and then you may go into extra innings. There is a lot of running in baseball. Baseball equipment includes: bats, balls, gloves, and cleats. Baseball is played on grass and astro-turf.

Golf is an individual sport. The object of the game is to hit the little ball with the club as few times as possible to get it into the hole. There is a lot of walking in golf. Golfers need clubs, balls, and cleats. Golf is played on grass courses, unless you're playing miniature gold. That's played on Astro-turf or green cement.

Similarities: _____

_____

_____

_____

_____

Differences: _____

_____

_____

_____

_____

_____

Name: _____ **Date:** _____

Come to the Cooper Costume Bash!

Saturday, October 27th
from 8:00-11:00
at the Cooper's House

Spooky foods and drinks will be served, including spider web cookies, spaghetti intestine stew, and bubbling cauldron punch!
You can also bring a frightening dish!

Listen to an all-ghoul quartet playing top hits from the Grateful Dead and the Mummies.

Prizes will be awarded for the scariest couple and most interesting individual.

You are invited to Alice's 10th Birthday Bonanza!

Saturday, October 27th
from 12:00-4:00

There will be lots of your favorite foods including pizza and hot dogs!

Gonzo the clown will be there to do magic tricks and take kids for rides on his pony, Pete.

The party is at Big Beach, so there's lots of room for all!

There will also be a DJ!

Hope you can come!

1. When does the costume bash take place? _____

2. When does the birthday party take place? _____

3. What foods will be at the Cooper's? _____

4. What foods will be at Alice's birthday party? _____ _____

5. Which party will have pony rides? _____

6. Which party will have live music? _____

7. Where are the Mummies playing? _____

8. Which party might put a little sand in your shoes? _____

9. Where will you see Gonzo? _____

10. Which party would you attend? Why? _____

_____

New York City

New York City was settled by the Dutch in the 1600s and is the largest city in the United States. It is the center of world finance, communications, and global business. New York City is unique because of its extremely diverse population, its hundreds of tall buildings, its huge central business district, its extensive public transportation system, and its more than 400 separate neighborhoods. The city's concert houses, museums, galleries, and theaters are world-renown. Manhattan Island sits in the Atlantic Ocean and has long been an important shipping port. The present population of New York City is about 7,500,000.

London

London is the capital of the United Kingdom. London is situated in southeastern England along the Thames River. With a population of just under 7 million, London is by far the largest city in Europe. This fact has been true since the 17th century. In the 19th century it was the largest and most influential city in the world, the center of culture and business. Although it is no longer #1 in the world, London is still one of the world's major financial and cultural capitals.

Similarities: _____

_____

_____

_____

_____

Differences: _____

_____

_____

_____

_____

Name: _____   **Date:** _____

Miss Mabel Marble, Head Mistress at Meadow School for Little Ladies:

It was nearly 11:20 on the night of October 5th. I had just rolled my hair in curlers and was about to fasten my night bonnet when I heard a noise that sounded very much like a shower of rain; however, the forecast had not predicted rain and I smelled no moisture in the air. Still the trickling sound continued. I parted the curtains to see a frightening occurrence—sand flying up, out of the playground sandbox, and landing on the roof of the school. I also saw Loretta Fay Flowers near the sandbox, pointing up to the sky, directing the sand, as if she had magical powers in her fingertips. I have always known there was something strange about that child. Something a good scolding has been unable to cure. She was purposely trying to cover the school building in sand.

Loretta Fay Flowers, Eleven-Year-Old Student at Meadow School for Little Ladies:

On October 5th at 11:20, I was awakened by a strange sound—the sound of sand flying from the sandbox in the school playground onto the roof of the school building. I ran outside to get a better look. I saw Miss Mabel Marble looking out the window of her bedroom. She had a strange twisted antenna in her hair, as if she were from another planet. She was pointing at the sand, making it fly through the sky onto the school building. There aren't many children who aren't terrified of Miss Mabel Marble, and now I know why. She's a space creature pretending to be a headmistress, so she can capture poor little girls and send them to another planet in outer space.

1. How are the stories the same? _____

_____

_____

2. How are the stories different? _____

_____

_____

3. Whose version do you believe? Why? _____

_____

_____

_____

Facts can be supported with evidence— opinions are all your own!

____ 1. Shakespeare is a famous playwright.

____ 2. He was born more than 400 hundred years ago.

____ 3. Shakespeare was born in England.

____ 4. England is a fun place to visit.

____ 5. I think Shakespeare's best play is *Hamlet*.

____ 6. There are ghosts in *Hamlet*.

____ 7. Shakespeare also wrote sonnets, which are short poems.

____ 8. Sonnets are better than plays.

____ 9. Everyone likes Shakespeare.

____ 10. Shakespeare wrote *Romeo and Juliet*.

____ 11. Everyone should read *Macbeth*.

____ 12. If he were living today, Shakespeare would be very rich.

____ 13. Many of Shakespeare's plays have been turned into movies.

____ 14. Shylock is a character in *The Merchant of Venice*.

____ 15. Shylock wants a pound of flesh. Yuck—he should be arrested!

Name: _____ **Date:** _____

1. George Washington was the first president of the United States.

2. He was a general in the Revolutionary War.

3. George Washington's wife was named Martha.

4. I think Martha is a pretty name.

5. George Washington never lived in the White House.

6. George Washington had no children.

7. Mount Vernon is the name of George Washington's residence.

8. Mount Vernon is located in Virginia.

9. Virginia is a cool place to go on vacation.

10. You should learn things when you go on vacation.

11. John Adams was the first vice president of the United States.

12. George Washington is called *The Father of Our Country*.

13. If still living, Washington would be elected president again.

14. Washington was born on February 22, 1732.

15. Washington died on December. 14, 1799, in Mount Vernon, Virginia.

Name: _____   **Date:** _____

Every action has a reaction! That's cause and effect.

Directions: *Read the following stories and answer the questions.*

Laura was the best diver at Midland Middle School. Saturday was the Western Regional Dive Championship. Laura's coach asked all the divers to get a good night's rest before the early morning competition. There was a chance Midland could earn a trophy if all the divers performed their best. Laura planned to go to sleep early on Friday night, but then she got a call from her friend, Sondra. Sondra invited Laura to a party. Laura went to the party and did not get to sleep until midnight. She overslept in the morning and missed the dive competition. She did not hear the phone ring when her coach and teammates tried to contact her. Midland did not win a trophy.

Cause: _____

_____

Effect: _____

_____

Andre wasn't the most popular kid at school. In fact, lots of kids made fun of him. Andre was as tall as a first-grader and he was nearly 12! Everyone in Andre's family was short, but that didn't stop them from being happy and successful. After school one Friday, the kids teased Andre so much he decided to walk home alone the long way. As Andre walked past an old building, he heard a cry for help. There was a tiny crawlspace with a woman standing in front of it crying. Her cat had crawled under the building and she couldn't reach him. The building was scheduled to be demolished. Without saying a word, Andre wiggled through the opening and rescued the cat. The woman was so thankful she gave Andre $100 and called the local newspapers to tell the story. Andre was a hero at school on Monday morning!

Cause: _____

_____

Effect: _____

_____

Name: _____   **Date:** _____

1. Effect: The beach's blazing sun scorched Lily's back and shoulders.
   Cause: _____

2. Effect: James avoided the school bus every day this week.
   Cause: _____

3. Effect: Mrs. Crabapple imparted a week of detention on the entire class.
   Cause: _____

4. Effect: Cindy appealed for lunch money from Lisa.
   Cause: _____

5. Effect: Billy's aroma reminds me of a skunk.
   Cause: _____

6. Effect: Matt swore he'd never consume another raw egg, no matter who dared him!
   Cause: _____

7. Effect: Jenny's sister Carol concealed her new wardrobe from Jenny.
   Cause: _____

8. Effect: Kevin's mother gave the directive: no television on school nights!
   Cause: _____

9. Effect: Spot chewed off most of the hair on his once fluffy tail.
   Cause: _____

10. Effect: The living room smelled of rotten eggs.
    Cause: _____

11. Effect: The Smith family arrived at the movie theater an hour too early.
    Cause: _____

12. Effect: The bottom of the frying pan was scorched and the food was ruined.
    Cause: _____

13. Effect: Lisa walked home from school alone in the rain.
    Cause: _____

14. Effect: Luke Likeable was elected class president by a 12-1 landslide.
    Cause: _____

15. Effect: Timmy was intrigued by the letter he received from his uncle.
    Cause: _____

Name: _____ **Date:** _____

Ask yourself questions about the characters as you read. It will help you get to know them.

Directions: *Read the paragraphs and then answer the character questions below.*

Tyson, Bull, and Ham have been business associates since kindergarten. They call themselves *The Money Magnets*. What an amazingly successful time they have had earning cash! From selling candy bars, to newspapers, to mowing lawns and raking leaves, the three are a motivated, triumphant team of savvy entrepreneurs. And they are only in the sixth grade!

The trio lives in a small, isolated town where kids often complain of monotonous summers. From that, an idea was born. This summer *The Money Magnets* are hosting a fair on the outskirts of town. Ham's father donated his vacant lot to the endeavor. There will be rides, entertainment, food, and fun for all ages. Each of the boys has his own particular talent to contribute. Tyson is great with numbers and math, so he is handling all of the event's finances. Bull is the most physically fit and enjoys the construction and design aspect of creating the fair. Finally, Ham is the group's entertainer! He hires the help, performs in the shows, and keeps everyone smiling!

1. If you were having trouble with geometry, whom might you ask for assistance?
   _____

2. The school is looking for volunteers to rebuild the old playground, who in the team would be best for the job? _____

3. Who might capture the lead in the school play? _____

4. Based on what you know about The Money Magnets, will the summer fair venture be a success? _____ Why? _____

5. How did Ham's father help the boys? _____

Now use your imagination—turn the clock ahead ten years. Write a short newspaper article about the business accomplishments of Tyson, Bull, and Ham. Use the back of this paper to continue your story.

_____

_____

_____

_____

Name: _____   **Date:** _____

Peter Pan by J.M. Barrie is a classic tale that has been enjoyed by children around the world for more than 100 years. The colorful characters make the story so wonderful. If you've read the book, this assignment will be a cinch—just search your memory for the answers. If not, get the book, read it, and enjoy!

Give one fact about each of the characters listed below.

Peter: _____

Wendy: _____

Michael: _____

John: _____

Tinkerbell: _____

Captain Hook: _____

The Lost Boys: _____

Nana: _____

Mrs. Darling: _____

Mr. Darling: _____

Now choose your favorite character from any story and fill in the 5 W's below. When you're done, write a short paragraph about your favorite character on the back of this page.

Who: _____

_____

What: _____

_____

When: _____

_____

Where: _____

_____

Why: _____

_____

Name: _____   **Date:** _____

Directions: *Use the results of the marathon to determine facts and draw conclusions.*

Riverdale High School held its annual Marathon on Saturday. Here are the results:

Kerri	finished 1st in 4:18.27
James	finished 2nd in 4:18.29
Sammy	finished 3rd in 4:35.01
Marco	finished 10 minutes after Sammy
Jenny	finished 8 minutes and 30 seconds after Sammy
Chris	walked the entire race in 7:43:15
Mattie	was disqualified for taking a ride on the back of her brother's bike
Azul	twisted his ankle at the 10-mile mark and was taken to the nurse
Victor	had blisters on all of his toes, but finished before Chris and Olive
Olive	did not finish last in this, her first marathon

1. Who was disqualified for cheating? _____

2. Who sustained an injury and had to quit? _____

3. Who sustained an injury but did not quit? _____

4. Who finished directly behind Sammy? _____

5. How many students finished the race? _____

6. Who did not run the race? _____

7. How long after the first finisher did the last finisher complete the marathon? _____

8. How much before Sammy did James finish? _____

9. Based on the times of the first two finishers, what conclusions can you make about their performances? Give a play-by-play of the final home stretch. _____

_____

10. List the runners in the order in which they finished: _____

_____

Name: _____ **Date:** _____

Mrs. Menders wanted to know how much time her students spent reading during the week. She asked each individual student, and their remarks are listed below.

Reading Poll:	Reading Materials:
Molly reads 4 nights a week for 20 minutes a day.	Fiction books
Sharon reads twice a week for 50 minutes a day.	Magazines, chapter books
Peter reads once a week for 45 minutes.	Textbook
Maribeth reads 5 nights a week for 10 minutes a day.	Library books
Carl reads 3 times a week for 1 hour a day.	Chapter books
Charlie reads every other day for 2 hours.	Chapter books
Naomi reads 100 minutes weekly.	Magazines, books
Eric reads for 15 minutes daily.	Textbooks
Norman reads about 10 minutes every 3 days.	Cereal boxes

1. Which child reads the most in a week? _____

2. Which child reads the least in a week? _____

3. Which children read the same amount in a week? _____

4. Who seems to enjoy reading? _____

   How can you tell? _____

5. Who doesn't enjoy reading? _____

   Why do you say that? _____

6. Why do you think Norman only reads for 10 minutes a day? _____

   _____

7. Whose reading habit are you most similar to? _____

8. Whose reading habit would you like to have? _____

   Why? _____

Name: _____   **Date:** _____

To make an inference is to come to a conclusion after considering __all__ the facts.

Directions: Look closely at the picture below, then answer the following questions about the picture.

1. What is going on in the picture? _____

_____

2. How do you think the mother feels? _____

_____

3. What is the son hiding? _____

4. Why is he hiding something? _____

_____

5. What clues lead you to believe that? _____

_____

6. What do you think will happen if his mother or father finds his napkin? _____

_____

_____

Name: _____   **Date:** _____

Directions: Wendy is manager of customer service at ABC Products. She received the following letters from customers. Read the letters and answer the questions. All letters must receive an immediate reply. Write a response to each customer on the back of this page.

Dear ABC People:

Your Water-Detection Wand is a farce and not worth the wire hanger it's made out of, let alone the $99.97 I paid! You promised I would be able to find water. Well, I haven't found so much as a puddle! The blasted thing keeps leading me to cactus! I already have a yard full of cactus! It gets pretty hot and dry out where I live in the Arizona desert and I need a waterfinder that actually works. I want my money back! I also want compensation for all the time I spent using your worthless device.

Sincerely,
Sandy Shore

Dear Customer Service at ABC:

I need some assistance with a gift I recently received. My grandson bought me a Clap-O-Phone for my 87th birthday. According to the directions, if I want to make a phone call, all I need do is clap out the numbers I desire dialed. That isn't as simple as it may sound, especially when the number I most frequently dial is that of my Turf Accountant at: 989-9998. It takes me exactly 17 minutes to make that many claps, more if I forget my place. I was wondering if you have a speed-dial attachment I can purchase. My hands are aching.

Thank you,
Dick T. Fine

Dear Sir or Madam:

I recently purchased your Wizzo- Matic Kitchen Wisk and I am thoroughly satisfied! I have never been able to make egg-whites peak so high before. My lemon chiffon pies are a sensation, thanks to your fabulous product.

Sincerely,
Abe Buffet

1. Which customer is most pleased with their product? List words that indicate this.

    _____

2. Which product doesn't appear to be functioning properly? Why? _____

    _____

3. How many claps would Mr. Fine have to make to call his Turf Accountant? _____

4. What do you know about cactus plants that might help Sandy Shore? _____

    _____

5. Which product would you like to own? Why? _____

    _____

Directions: *Read or recall the story of the Three Little Pigs and then answer the questions below. Write "yes" on the blank if the sentence is something you can infer from the story. Write "no" if it is not.*

1. The wolf has bad breath. _____

2. One little pig makes a house out of straw. _____

3. Another little piggy uses sticks to build his house. _____

4. The wisest piggy likes to read architecture books. _____

5. The wolf is hungry. _____

6. The best-built house is brick. _____

7. The story takes place in July. _____

8. One piggy saves the other three. _____

9. The wolf recently had an encounter with Little Red Riding Hood. _____

10. The wolf frightens the pigs. _____

11. The piggy with the straw house bought his furniture on sale. ____

12. The wolf was sorry he had a taste for pork. _____

13. Mr. Goat watched the wolf blow down the stick house and said nothing. _____

14. The wolf was heard saying, "Little pig, little pig, let me in or I'll huff, and puff, and blow your house down!" _____

15. The wolf should get a job blowing up balloons at the circus. _____

Reading Comprehension • Saddleback Publishing, Inc. ©2002   104   3 Watson, Irvine, CA 92618•Phone (888)SDL-BACK•www.sdlback.com

1. I'm running late. I'd better let my mother know that I won't be home in time for dinner. What's the quickest way to get in contact?

     a. telephone   b. letter   c. messenger

2. I'm sending invitations to all my computer friends. I'm sending these invitations without stamps. How are they being sent?

     a. by postcard   b. via e-mail   c. by fax

3. My sister was driving 45 in a 25 zone. She heard a siren. Who do you think is following her?

     a. an ice cream truck   b. my dad   c. the police

4. Peggy set the picnic table. Everyone had a decorative napkin and paper plate. Suddenly a huge gust of wind tore through the park. What happened to the settings?

     a. they blew away   b. Peggy managed to hold them down   c. the napkins got wet

5. Rudy's hair keeps falling in his eyes. His father took him to a place with swivel chairs and lots of mirrors. The manager is sharpening scissors. Where is Rudy?

     a. the barber   b. the movies   c. a hardware store

6. There's a terrible smell in the car. Mike was in a hurry yesterday when he came back from fishing. What did he leave in the trunk?

     a. his fishing rod   b. the bait   c. his sneakers

7. Lucy is afraid of heights. She refuses to go on which ride at the fair?

     a. the merry-go-round   b. the bumper cars   c. the Ferris wheel

8. Tanya loves attention and has a wonderful voice. Fondue Palace has karaoke on Saturday nights. Why does Tanya go there every week?

     a. she loves fondue   b. she enjoys singing for a crowd c. she has a gift certificate

9. The sun was blocked for three minutes. You had to wear special glasses to see the event. What happened?

     a. a lunar eclipse   b. a solar eclipse   c. a storm was approaching

10. Alice covered herself in sunscreen. Where was she going?

     a. to the movies   b. to school   c. to the beach

Name: _____   Date: _____

Details, details, details... read carefully and you won't miss anything important.

Directions: *Read the advertisements and fill in the details.*

Don't let pests ruin your picnic! Zap-Bands are the revolutionary way to enjoy outdoor events without scratching and itching. Just place a Zap-Band below your wristwatch or above your shoe. The invisible barrier is created immediately. No smell, no stain, no mess!

1. What type of pests might bother you at a picnic? _____

2. On what two parts of your body can you wear the Zap-Bands? _____

3. What season would you most likely need a Zap-Band? _____

4. What does the barrier look and smell like? _____

5. Will Zap-Bands stain your clothes? _____

FullJug is the winner of the New Products of the Year Award for Excellence. Developed with thirsty people in mind, FullJug removes moisture from the air and traps it for later consumption. You never have to refill FullJug! Thanks to the patented ever-fill technology, one gallon of water is always available for consumption. Humidity factors dictate how quickly FullJug replenishes itself. The more humidity, the quicker the refill time.

1. What is FullJug? _____

2. Who might want to purchase this product? _____

3. Consumption means? _____

4. Where would FullJug refill itself quicker—in a tropical rain forest or the desert?_____

5. How much water does FullJug hold? _____

Have you ever run out of tape, right in the middle of wrapping a gift or sealing a package? It's very frustrating! Not any more with Stretch Tape. Now you can turn that last inch of tape into a yard or more! Just pull the tape until you have the desired amount. There's no limit to how far you can pull Stretch Tape. A roll of Stretch Tape can last for years. With our introductory offer, you get five rolls of Stretch Tape for two easy payments of only $39.95! Hurry, supplies are limited.

1. What is Stretch Tape? _____

2. Would you buy Stretch Tape? Why? _____

3. What will it cost you for five rolls of Stretch Tape in this offer? _____

4. What do they mean by "supplies are limited?" _____

5. Introductory means? _____

Name: _____ **Date:** _____

My name is Hillary Gordon, and my parents bought me tickets to the circus for my 12th birthday. "I'm going to the circus, going to the circus!" My brother Bill threatened to gag me with his smelly socks if I said the word circus one more time.

On Saturday, my family eagerly piled into the car and headed downtown to the Convention Center to the circus. Bill was fussing that he had to sit next to Auntie Lupe and her old dog Snickers. Snickers suffers from incontinence— Auntie Lupe always carries lots of damp towels. Bill is such a complainer.

As we entered the circus, I could smell the pungent aroma of popcorn and candy. When we arrived at our seats, I asked my father to buy some cotton candy. Before Dad could pass it down the aisle to me, Bill grabbed a huge handful of my pink cotton candy and shoved it into his mouth. He then took my paper cone and kept poking poor Snickers in the back of the head. Auntie Lupe didn't bring enough towels to clean up the consequences of Bill's pestering. The people behind us changed seats.

My favorite act was the Amazing Armando Trapeze Family. They could swing and flip and catch each other's toes in mid-air. Bill said he could swallow fire while swinging from the livingroom drapes and promised to prove it when we got home. I bet Bill $2 he couldn't get three feet off the ground without singeing his eyebrows or being walloped with Mother's broom. He took my bet.

Let's say that the evening's events topped the big top—six fire trucks responded to a neighbor's call of a flying torch in our living room. When it was over, Bill was hairless and in loads of trouble.

1. How would you describe Hillary? Use details from the story to support your description.

_____

2. Why didn't Bill want to sit next to Snickers? _____

3. Why did the people behind the Gordon family change seats? _____

4. Use three adjectives, not in the story, to describe Bill. _____

5. What's so amazing about the Amazing Armando Trapeze Family? _____

6. Another word for big top is _____

7. Do you think Hillary won the bet with Bill? Why? _____

8. What did Hillary think was more exciting than the circus? _____

9. What was the flying torch? _____

10. Tell this story from Bill's point of view. _____

Directions: *Read the story below. Then number the events in the order they happened.*

Detective Declan was called to investigate a robbery at Rings & Things. When he arrived at the store, people were running around frantically and a policeman was taping off the area with bright yellow ribbon, which read: CRIME SCENE. Authorities didn't want anyone near the site until Detective Declan had done his investigation. "We've been waiting for you," grumbled the sheriff.

Detective Declan walked into the store; it was dark. He tried to turn on the lights, but they didn't work. He took a couple of steps; he heard the sound of glass breaking beneath his feet. He'd found the broken light bulb. He reached into his pocket, took out his flashlight, and shined it on the floor. In the spotlight, Detective Declan could see watches, ladies rings, bracelets, and necklaces that had been left behind in haste. Some had spots of pink on them. He also saw a pink streak across the display case glass. It faintly smelled of paint.

With that, Detective Declan walked outside into the bright sunlight. The Rings & Things cashier, Ms. Pearl, was sitting on the sidewalk; she had not yet been questioned about the robbery. Detective Declan looked down at her well-manicured hands. Two pink nails were visibly smudged. "Ms. Pearl," smiled Declan. "Perhaps it would have been prudent for you to wait until your manicure had fully dried." Case closed!

a. _____ He went outside to interview, Ms. Pearl, the cashier.

b. _____ Detective Declan accidentally stepped on a light bulb.

c. _____ He noticed pink smudges.

d. _____ Detective Declan saw jewelry on the floor, left in haste.

e. _____ The police needed Detective Declan's help.

f. _____ Detective Declan solved the case!

g. _____ Detective Declan walked onto the crime scene.

h. _____ Detective Declan used his flashlight to illuminate the crime scene.

i. _____ The crime scene was taped off with yellow ribbon.

j. _____ The sheriff was waiting for Detective Declan.

Name: _____

Date: _____

My mom taught me how to make her famous chocolate chip cookie ice cream pie. It's my favorite! The notion of making a pie from scratch sounds simple, but there are many steps involved, if you want your end product to be perfectly delicious.

The first thing my mom does is to write a list of pie ingredients. Then she checks the refrigerator, freezer, and pantry to see if she has the necessary items. If not, she makes a grocery list, and takes a quick trip to the supermarket.

Chocolate chip cookie ice cream pie requires:

1 16 oz package of chocolate chip cookies (or homemade)	$\frac{1}{2}$ cup softened butter
1 cup hot fudge topping	2 quarts chocolate chip ice cream
1 cup of whipped cream	12 cherries

Once you have all the ingredients, you are ready to begin. First, Mom crushes $\frac{3}{4}$ of the cookies into crumbs. Then she adds the crumbs to the softened butter and presses them into the bottom of a deep pie plate. She places the remaining cookie crumbs around the edge of the plate for decoration. Next, Mom spreads most of the fudge topping over the crust. She saves some for the top of the pie. When that part is complete, it's time to put the pie into the freezer for 15 minutes.

While the crust is freezing, Mom puts one quart of ice cream in the microwave for 45 seconds. This helps to soften the ice cream. After that, she takes the crust out of the freezer and spreads the ice cream over the fudge and cookie crust.

Finally, Mom scoops the rest of the ice cream into balls and arranges them on top of the pie. Once again she freezes the pie, this time overnight. The rest of the fudge topping, whipped cream, cookie crumbs, and cherries go on top before serving! Delicious!

a. _____ My Mom goes to the supermarket and buys what she will need.

b. _____ Then she puts the fudge on the crust.

c. _____ She puts the pie in the freezer for 15 minutes.

d. _____ Finally, she tops the pie with whipped cream, cookie crumbs, and cherries!

e. _____ Next she puts the ice cream on top of the fudge.

f. _____ Then she begins making the pie.

g. _____ My Mom makes a list of the ingredients she will need.

h. _____ First, she crushes the cookies to make the crust.

i. _____ After that, my Mom puts the pie in the freezer overnight.

j. _____ It's time to eat the pie.

Name: _____   **Date:** _____

Everyone has his or her own view of the world. Authors' share their point of view through their writing.

Directions: *Read the story below. Then answer the questions.*

Mom joined Dad on a business trip last weekend. Grandma Tucker came to stay with us while they were away. My brother and I were excited because we don't often get to spend time alone with Grandma Tucker. Besides being a fun, beautiful, and thoughtful woman, Grandma Tucker has a remarkably creative imagination. She can make really amazing toys out of almost nothing. My brother Will and I brag about her to all of our friends.

As soon as my parents departed, Grandma's talents shifted into gear. She collected scraps of fabric from Mom's sewing basket and made new dresses for my dolls. Then she wound string around strips of plastic bags and made parachutes for Will's army men. By the time my parents returned, Will and I had a new and improved collection of toy accessories. Grandma Tucker is even more amazing than I remembered!

1. What does the author think of her grandmother coming to visit? _____

2. What does the author think of her grandmother's talent? _____

3. List adjectives the author uses to describe her grandmother. _____
   _____

4. List adjectives the author uses to describe her grandmother's talents. _____
   _____

5. Based on what you've read, how would you describe the author? _____
   _____

6. Is there someone whose talents impress you? Write about that person on the lines below.
   _____
   _____
   _____
   _____
   _____
   _____

Name: _____   **Date:** _____

First Person: Sentences that include I, me, my, we, mine, our
My name is Harold. I like playing Grubbish in my spare time. Grubbish is a game played with cans and balls. Our neighborhood park has a Grubbish team, and I have been elected the captain.

1. _____
2. _____
3. _____

Second Person: Sentences that include you, yourself
Grubbish is a game played with cans and balls. You have to kick the small balls into cans. This is a task-oriented competition done all by yourself as you compete against the clock.

1. _____
2. _____
3. _____

Third Person: Sentences that include he, she, and proper names, such as Jack
Jack plays first-string smasher for the Pixy Park Grubbish team. He has been on the team for nearly three years. His sister Mandy is also on the team, although she is new to the sport.

1. _____
2. _____
3. _____

Omniscient: This all-knowing voice can get into the mind of the characters. Sentences contain character secrets as well as feelings and emotions.
Harold felt a chill travel up his spine as he prepared to take the field for the Grubbish match. He was nervous, and he hoped no one could detect that fact. As if nerves weren't enough to deal with, the weather got worse. From the corner of his eye, Harold could see a large, dark cloud creeping across the horizon. If only he'd taken along a raincoat.

1. _____
2. _____
3. _____

Name: _____   **Date:** _____

Take a look at the view from the character's perspective. Point-of-view depends on who's viewing the point!

Directions: How would your two favorite fictional book kid characters answer the questions below? Crawl into their minds and decide. If you need to re-familiarize yourself with these characters, first make a trip to the library.

Character Name: _____

1. How old are you? _____

2. Do you live with your parents? _____

3. How do you feel about the people you live with? Why? _____

4. Who is your best friend? _____

5. What activities do you enjoy? _____

6. What do you want to be when you grow up? _____

7. Do you go to school? _____

8. What makes you sad? _____

9. Describe an adventure you've had. _____

Character Name: _____

10. How old are you? _____

11. Do you live with your parents? _____

12. How do you feel about the people you live with? Why? _____

13. Who is your best friend? _____

14. What activities do you enjoy? _____

15. What do you want to be when you grow up? _____

16. Do you go to school? _____

17. What makes you sad? _____

18. Describe an adventure you've had. _____

Name: _____   **Date:** _____

A. Sharks: Sharks are the worst animals in the ocean, and I don't see any reason why they exist. I think every fisherman that catches a shark should be paid $100 by the state Fish & Game Council. One time I was swimming and a shark approached me. I was in shallow water and stood very still. Nothing happened, but it made me realize that sharks are very dangerous menaces!

> By Mandy

1. How does Mandy feel about sharks? Why? _____

_____

2. List three adjectives that describe Mandy's viewpoint. _____

_____

B. Sharks: Sharks are beautiful creatures that have survived and thrived in the sea for millions of years. Movies and television have unfairly portrayed these humble creatures as vicious killers, when in actuality they are scavengers doing what comes natural for their survival. I believe that anyone who kills a shark should be fined $1,000 and sent to a class on sharks so they can learn what is true and what is folklore about these amazing fish!

> By Fletcher

1. How does Fletcher feel about sharks? Why? _____

_____

2. List three adjectives that describe Fletcher's viewpoint. _____

_____

C. Sharks: I have only seen sharks in the movies and on television. I think some of them are evil and others are harmless. I know lots of people hate sharks and others want to protect them. Therefore, there should be a compromise. All sharks should be captured and put into one ocean—that way people will know where they are and can avoid being attacked.

> By Eva

1. How does Eva feel about sharks? Why? _____

_____

2. List three adjectives that describe Eva's viewpoint. _____

_____

Name: _____   Date: _____

Story events have significance and it's up to the reader to read carefully and find the important information.

Directions: *Read the letter carefully and answer the questions.*

Dear Diary,
It is 1940, and I am a Jewish teenager living in Poland. I am 14. I am extremely frightened by some of the talk that I have heard about Adolf Hitler and his plan to exterminate the Jewish population. My parents have tried to calm my fears. They tell my brother and me that the world is too civilized for such a thing to happen, and that it would be impossible for Hitler to wipe out an entire population of people. Despite their attempts to make me feel better, I remain frightened. Why must I wear a yellow armband with the Star of David? I do not want attention drawn to me. I am Polish, just like all of the other kids in my class. It is not fair to be considered different. Some of my friends no longer speak to me.

I am fortunate to have you, my diary friend, to confide in. I would go mad if I had to keep all of my emotions bottled up in my body any longer. I do not know whom to trust with my thoughts. The world is not what it was only last year. I suspect everyone of ill doing; my mother says I am becoming paranoid. Until I write again, I remain.

Faithfully,
Margo

1. What year is it? _____

2. How old is this character? _____

3. Who is Margo writing to? _____

4. Why is she frightened? _____

5. What do her parents say about her fears? Why? _____

_____

6. What must Margo wear that makes her feel different? _____

7. How do Margo's friends treat her? _____

8. Why is Margo becoming paranoid? _____

9. Does Margo have any siblings? _____

10. How would you feel in Margo's situation? _____

Name: _____ **Date:** _____

Read the passage and answer the questions. Use your dictionary and encyclopedia for help.

From 1920 until about 1930 an extraordinary outburst of creative activity among black Americans occurred in all fields of art, music, and literature. Beginning as a series of literary deliberations in New York City's Greenwich Village and Harlem sections of town, this African American cultural movement became known as the Harlem Renaissance. More than a literary movement and more than a social revolt against racism, the Harlem Renaissance was the rebirth of African Americans; it redefined African American expression. Black Americans were encouraged to celebrate their heritage and use their talents to express themselves creatively.

One of the factors contributing to the rise of the Harlem Renaissance was the great migration of African Americans from the south to northern cities such as New York City, Chicago, and Washington, D.C. between the years 1919 and 1926. Education and social status were important to these burgeoning arts and the fruits of their creation are still revered today.

1. What was the Harlem Renaissance? _____

_____

2. What does renaissance mean? _____

_____

3. Where did the Harlem Renaissance take place? _____

_____

4. What was a factor contributing to the rise of the Harlem Renaissance? _____

_____

5. Do a little research. Name an artist, a musician, and writer that flourished during the Harlem Renaissance. _____

_____

_____

Name: _____   **Date:** _____

**Main characters are the stars of the show!
See if you can locate them below.**

The Ant and the Chrysalis

An ant nimbly running about in the sunshine in search of food came across a chrysalis that was very near its time of change. The chrysalis moved its tail, and thus attracted the attention of the ant, who then saw for the first time that it was alive. "Poor, pitiable animal!" cried the ant disdainfully. "What a sad fate is yours! While I can run hither and thither, at my pleasure, and, if I wish, ascend the tallest tree, you lie imprisoned here in your shell, with power only to move a joint or two of your scaly tail." The chrysalis heard all this, but did not try to make any reply. A few days after, when the ant passed that way again, nothing but the shell remained. Wondering what had become of its contents, he felt himself suddenly shaded and fanned by the gorgeous wings of a beautiful butterfly. "Behold in me," said the butterfly, "your much-pitied friend! Boast now of your powers to run and climb as long as you can get me to listen." So saying, the butterfly rose in the air, and, borne along and aloft on the summer breeze, was soon lost to the sight of the ant forever.

1. Who is the main character of the story? Why? _____
   _____

2. Underline the quote that would be true for the main character?
   a. Love is blind.
   b. Appearances are deceptive.
   c. All is fair in love and war.

3. Add a paragraph to the end of this fable. How did the ant feel after the butterfly departed? Why? What was the butterfly thinking as he took off? Why? _____

   _____
   _____
   _____
   _____

Name: _____   **Date:** _____

Read the Aesop Fable and answer the questions about the main character. Use the back of this page if needed.

An old man on the point of death summoned his sons around him to give them some parting advice. He ordered his servants to bring in a bundle of sticks, and said to his eldest son "Break it." The son strained and strained, but with all his efforts was unable to break the bundle. The other sons also tried, but none of them was successful. "Untie the bundle," said the father, "and each of you take a stick." When they had done so, he called out to them "Now, break," and each stick was easily broken. "You see my meaning," said their father.

1. Why should the father be considered the main character? _____

2. How would you describe the father? Why? _____

_____

3. What was the father's meaning? _____

_____

4. Which would make the best title for this fable? Why?
   a. Union Gives Strength
   b. Safety in Numbers
   c. Age is Wisdom

5. Choose one of the topics below and write your own short fable.
   a. Do not attempt too much at once.
   b. Necessity is the mother of invention.
   c. Little friends may prove great friends.

_____

_____

_____

_____

_____

_____

_____

Name: _____   **Date:** _____

Where did it happen? The answer is always found in the story's setting.

1. The waves crashed gently along the sandy shore as the sun blazed down from above. Bathers in bright colors frolicked and laughed and splashed one another playfully.
   Setting: _____

2. Enormous trees blocked the sky above. Only the sound of parrots squawking could be heard through the rush of falling rain. The humidity would not break, even after the storm ceased. **Setting:** _____

3. I pushed my squeaky metal cart down the long aisle. Cans and boxes of food lined both sides. Children begged their weary mothers for treats and sweets. A voice from above announced a sale on boiled ham. **Setting:** _____

4. Diamonds, rubies, emeralds, and gold glittered inside the locked cabinet. A well-dressed woman smiled and asked if I wanted to view any of the merchandise. I pointed to an ornate ring in the front row. She took a set of keys from her pocket and opened the case. **Setting:** _____

5. The headstones were weathered and worn. I could barely decipher the names of the people who lay beneath. Some fear this place, especially at night. However, I enjoy the peacefulness of earth, and stone, and eternal rest. **Setting:** _____

6. The ocean was calm and the wind completely still. The captain ordered his men to drop sails. **Setting:** _____

7. Car #44 roared down the track past the rest of the drivers. Suddenly, there was a BANG! One of #44's tires was in shreds and the car was careening out of control.
   Setting: _____

8. The old tiger looked wearily at me through the bars of his cage. The sign read PLEASE DO NOT FEED, but I decided to share my hot dog with the poor fellow anyway.
   Setting: _____

9. We could see planet Earth from our cockpit window. It looked so tiny from way up here. **Setting:** _____

10. The bell rang. Harriet heard it as she leapt off the bus and ran toward the front doors. She hated to be late for Mrs. Unger's class! **Setting:** _____

Name: _____   **Date:** _____

Example:

Hockey game: The empty arena was ice-cold. The players entered carrying their sticks and skates. They put on their protective gear before stepping onto the slick ice.

1. **Movie theater:** _____
   _____
   _____
   _____

2. **Restaurant:** _____
   _____
   _____
   _____

3. **Golf course:** _____
   _____
   _____
   _____

4. **Museum:** _____
   _____
   _____
   _____

5. **A hot-air balloon:** _____
   _____
   _____
   _____

6. **A castle:** _____
   _____
   _____
   _____

Name: _____ **Date:** _____

Want a hint? — Think about what you already know to order events by time. You can do it!

Directions: *Read the sentences and select the correct time each took place. Refer to the choices below.*

Revolutionary War	Civil War	Prehistoric	Future	1960s
March 15, 44 B.C.	Old West	Present	1492	1990s

1. Thanks to his habit of sharing the proceeds from his crimes with the widows and children of men killed or ruined by bankers and cattle barons, Butch Cassidy earned a reputation as the Robin Hood of his time.
   Time _____

2. A day known as the Ides of March, Julius Caesar entered the Senate House. As Caesar entered the Senate, he was assassinated.
   Time _____

3. General George Washington looked out among his troops. Famine, frost, and exhaustion was taking its toll on these brave men.
   Time _____

4. Giant reptiles called dinosaurs roamed the Earth long before humans.
   Time _____

5. Lincoln sat in his study. His face was drawn and gaunt, a mirror of the turmoil he felt inside as his country battled—brother against brother.
   Time _____

6. The War in Vietnam raged, and the Beatles played on nearly every radio and jukebox in the world.
   Time _____

7. Christopher Columbus left Spain for his first voyage.
   Time _____

8. Bill Clinton defeats George Bush and becomes the next president of the United States.
   Time _____

9. Houses on the moon, trips to Venus, robots that do your homework.
   Time _____

10. Every kid seems to own a DVD player and a cell phone.
    Time _____

Name: _____   **Date:** _____

Scan the descriptions to help you understand the plot or main idea of the story.

Directions: *Read these famous story plots and then name the story. Unscramble the puzzle if you need help.*

1. Mean stepmother treats beautiful stepdaughter very cruelly. Beautiful stepdaughter gets even when she fits the shoe and marries the prince.

   Story_____ E R D E C I N A L L

2. Boy and girl fall in love. Their families feud. Boy and girl die tragically. Families make peace.

   Story_____ O O E M R & T E I L J U

3. A space creature is left behind by his shipmates. A little boy finds the space creature. The little boy returns the space creature to his ship.

   Story_____ T E

4. Seven dwarfs help a young woman hide from her evil stepmother. When she eats the poison apple, however, it takes the kiss of a prince to bring her back to life.

   Story_____ W O S N   H I W T E

5. A mermaid wants to be a human, and gets her wish.

   Story_____ E T T L I L   D I A M M R E

6. A puppet maker wants a son, and finally gets his wish.

   Story_____ N O C C H I P O I

7. A doctor who knows how to speak to animals causes quite a commotion.

   Story_____ R D   D L T O T E I L

8. A lion cub grows up to avenge the death of his father and restore his kingdom.

   Story_____ O N I L   G N K I

9. A likeable outlaw robs from the rich to give to the poor.

   Story_____ B R O I N   O O D H

10. Gorillas in the wilds of Africa raise a human baby.

    Story_____ R Z A A T N

Name: _____   **Date:** _____

A good author can inform, persuade, or entertain the reader. You can do this, too.

Directions: *Read the information passage below. Then fill in the boxes.*

Daniel Webster was the ninth born son of Ebenezer Webster, who was a farmer and tavern-keeper. Daniel was born in Salisbury, New Hampshire, on January 18, 1782. He was nicknamed "Black Dan" because of his jet-colored hair. When he was a child he was very ill and often bedridden. His family thought he wouldn't survive to adulthood. Daniel could do little except read. He soon fell in love with books. When Daniel was just fifteen he entered Dartmouth College. After graduating, he taught for a little while before working in a law office in Boston.

In 1807 Webster married and moved to Portsmouth. He became a lawyer in the fast-changing seaport. Though his law practice was an immediate success, Daniel did not socialize with the important people in his community. Daniel preferred evenings at home with his family.

Daniel Webster actively supported the pro-British Federalist Party. Webster was elected to the House of Representatives in 1817 and the Senate in 1827. This is where he earned his reputation as America's best orator. Webster eventually joined the Whig Party and served as Secretary of State under William Henry Harrison in 1841 and John Tyler until 1843. Webster also served as Secretary of State under Fillmore from 1850 until 1852. Although he strongly opposed slavery, Webster supported the Fugitive Slave Act in 1850. This angered the anti-slavery Whigs. Webster lost his presidential bid in 1852. Instead, Franklin Pierce got the nomination. Daniel Webster died on October 24, 1852.

Who: _____

What: _____

Where: _____

Important Information: _____
_____
_____

What I Learned: _____
_____
_____

Name: _____   **Date:** _____

When you write persuasively you are trying to get your reader to understand and agree with your point of view. Read the following tips for persuasive writing. Then choose a topic you care about and write your own persuasive piece. Some sample topics have been provided.

1. Choose a topic that matters to you.
2. Be sure to take a strong position.
3. Present convincing arguments in order to change the reader's mind.
4. Write in a clear and convincing manner.
5. Have at least three reasons and elaborate equally on all three.
6. Save the strongest reason as the last point: Save the best for last.
7. Do not take for granted that the reader understands your position. Clarify any statement you make.
8. Do not use needless repetitions.
9. Add details that support the position taken.
10. Give examples and be specific.
11. Organize ideas to flow logically.
12. Close appropriately by restating your point with a quick summary.

Possible Topics

- Kids should go to school only four days each week.
- School cafeterias need to improve lunches.
- Homework should be limited to one hour.
- Schools should go to a no-grades system.

_____

_____

_____

_____

_____

_____

_____

_____

_____

Name: _____   **Date:** _____

Every story and character has a mood.

Directions: *Analyze the mood of both paragraphs below. Then, answer the questions. Use the back of the page as needed.*

A. When Adam did not show up on time after school, his mother was frantic. She hastened to phone his best friend's house to see if he stopped there. At first Adam's voice on the other end of the line reassured her, but her relief soon turned to wrath. After she knew Adam was safe, she really let him have it for not checking in.

1. Is this paragraph suspenseful, humorous, mysterious, serious, or a combination of moods?

_____

2. Why or what makes you think this? _____

3. What picture came to mind as you read this paragraph? _____

4. How did you feel when you read the paragraph? _____

5. Suppose you could rewrite the paragraph to change its mood. What would you do to change it? _____

_____

B. It had been a grueling winter, but now spring was just around the corner. Carlotta decided that a garden would be just the thing to perk up everyone's spirits. Her grandfather had a green thumb, so she asked him to help her find the perfect spot in the yard. Mr. King found a sunny area near the rear of their property. Together, they enclosed it with a short mesh fence to keep out the rabbits and squirrels. Carlotta prepared the soil as her grandpa instructed, planted and watered her garden. By April, the plants had begun to sprout, and in May Carlotta's flowers began to bloom.

6. Is this paragraph suspenseful, humorous, happy, serious, or a combination of moods?

_____

7. Why or what makes you think this? _____

8. What picture came to mind as you read this paragraph? _____

9. How did you feel when you read the paragraph? _____

10. Suppose you could rewrite the paragraph to change its mood. What would you do to change it? _____

_____

Name: _____   **Date:** _____

1. I found out that my two best friends, Sherri and Kara, went skating at Bryant Park yesterday without ever calling to invite me! Instead, I sat at home all day playing tedious monster trucks with my baby brother, Gordon. My feelings are immensely crushed!

How do you think she felt? _____

Why? _____

2. While trying to study for my huge math test, both of my little bothersome brothers came into my bedroom, running and screaming and then began bouncing like acrobats on my bed. I yelled at them to get out immediately, but they ignored me and kept jumping. They threw pillows at my head and raced out of my bedroom, leaving it in shambles!

How do you think he felt? _____

Why? _____

3. My treasured fish, Bubbles, expired. My dad buried him in the backyard. Dad took his shovel from the garage and dug a hole in the corner yard beneath our willow tree. As I watched my dad, tears poured out of my eyes. Dad turned around, took the fish bowl from me and placed Bubbles inside the hole. Using his shovel again, my dad packed the hole with loose dirt.

How do you think he felt? _____

Why? _____

4. Everyday Gina walks home from school solo. When she arrives at her front door, she checks to see that no one is hiding in the bushes, then reaches into her backpack to retrieve her house keys and unlock the front door. Gina's parents work late and are never home before 7:00. One day Gina tried to unlock the front door, but to her astonishment it was ajar!

How do you think she felt? _____

Why? _____

Name: _____ **Date:** _____

It's really important to get the facts straight as you read. "Picturing" events in your mind will help you do this.

Directions: *Read the paragraph below. Then answer the following questions. Use the back of this page as needed.*

Eating balanced meals and exercising every day are important parts of a healthy lifestyle. Certain foods give your body vitamins it needs to grow, make energy, and stay fit. A good diet includes grains, vegetables, fruits, low-fat milk products, lean meats, fish, poultry, and dry beans. Try to avoid foods that are high in fat or sugar. Focus on the amount and types of foods you eat over a few days and try to eat a variety of different foods.

Exercise is also part of a healthy lifestyle, but safety is a very important concern when it comes to exercise, sports, and kids. About 250,000 children are hurt playing sports each year. Many injuries happen in unorganized games such as street football and backyard baseball, rather than in team sports like Little League and swimming competition. Sports on wheels, like skateboarding, bicycling, and roller-skating, can also be dangerous. Many kids wipe out on skateboards and skates each year and end up in the hospital with concussions and broken bones. Injuries are worse when safety equipment like helmets, kneepads, and wrist pads are not worn. Be smart—play safe and eat right.

1. What two things do you need to stay healthy? _____

2. What types of foods make up a healthy diet? _____

3. What types of foods should you avoid? _____ _____

4. How can you protect yourself from an injury when playing a sport? _____

_____

5. Why are sports with wheels sometimes dangerous? _____

_____

6. Think about what you have eaten in the last 24 hours. Make a list of all the foods and drinks. How do they measure up on the healthy scale? _____

7. What activities do you participate in? _____

8. List safety precautions you take when playing sports. _____

_____

Name: _____   **Date:** _____

One of the most feared dinosaurs in prehistoric times was the Tyrannosaurus Rex.

T-Rex, as it is commonly known, lived 65 million years ago. Other dinosaurs living at that same time were Triceratops, and Ankylosaurus. Fossils of the Tyrannosaurus Rex have been found in Montana.

This dinosaur was up to 40 feet long and stood 15 to 20 feet tall (about 3–4 people tall). Tyrannosaurus Rex weighed 10,000 to 14,000 pounds and had a huge head. The T-Rex had tiny arms and only 2 sharp-clawed fingers on each hand. Tyrannosaurus Rex walked and ran very fast on two huge back legs and balanced on sharp-clawed 3-toed feet. Archeologists and scientists claim that Tyrannosaurus Rex could run about 30 miles per hour! The T-Rex also had a thin, stiff, pointed tail that was powerful enough to knock down a larger dinosaur in battle. The mouth of a T-Rex was even scarier—it held 60 serrated teeth, each 9 inches long. When a tooth fell out, another tooth would quickly grow back in its place. Tyrannosaurus Rex could see and smell exceptionally well. A T-Rex often lived alone but would sometimes travel with another T-Rex. Like most reptiles, Tyrannosaurus Rex laid eggs. It is not known if the T-Rex took care of its young.

1. How long ago did the Tyrannosaurus Rex live? _____

_____

2. Where have T-Rex bones been found? _____

_____

3. How fast could a Tyrannosaurus Rex run? _____

_____

4. What would happen if T-Rex lost a tooth? _____

_____

5. How was the T-Rex similar to present-day reptiles? _____

_____

6. Pretend you are a T-Rex. What would be a typical day for you? _____

_____

Name: _____   **Date:** _____

A generalization is a simplification of a large topic. So, think carefully—what is one true thing you can say about all the information?

Directions: *Read each passage and then make a generalization about the topic discussed.*

1. Throughout time, dogs have been humans' useful and faithful servants. Dogs protect and defend homes, farms, and businesses, and also provide companionship to their owners. Dogs can be trained to be the ears and eyes of disabled humans; they can also entertain us in movies.

Generalization: _____

2. Most people know that humans cannot survive without water. However, did you know that 75% of Americans are chronically dehydrated? In many Americans, the thirst mechanism is so weak that it is often mistaken for hunger. Even mild dehydration will slow down your metabolism. One glass of water shut down midnight hunger pangs for almost 100% of dieters. Lack of water is the #1 trigger of daytime fatigue. A mere 2% drop in body water can trigger fuzzy short-term memory, trouble with basic math, and difficulty focusing on the computer screen or on a printed page. Go take a water break!

Generalization: _____

3. If you want to become proficient at something, practice makes perfect! Whether it is learning how to play a musical instrument or growing a vegetable garden, the tricks of the trade cannot be bought, only learned through patience and hard work. So when you set your sights on a skill, remember to keep your sights on the goal while you practice, practice, practice!

Generalization: _____

4. My brother and I have very different tastes in movies. When it's time to rent from the video store, we always argue. I prefer movies that have a riveting or dramatic story line. My brother, on the other hand, cares nothing for plots; all he wants is a good car chase or some monster gore. Luckily, our video store has 2-for-1 rentals on Thursdays. That way we both get what we want.

Generalization: _____

Name: _____ **Date:** _____

Directions: *For each generalization below, write three supporting sentences.*

1. Every child needs love.

2. Nothing is impossible.

3. Everything must come to an end.

4. The weather is unpredictable.

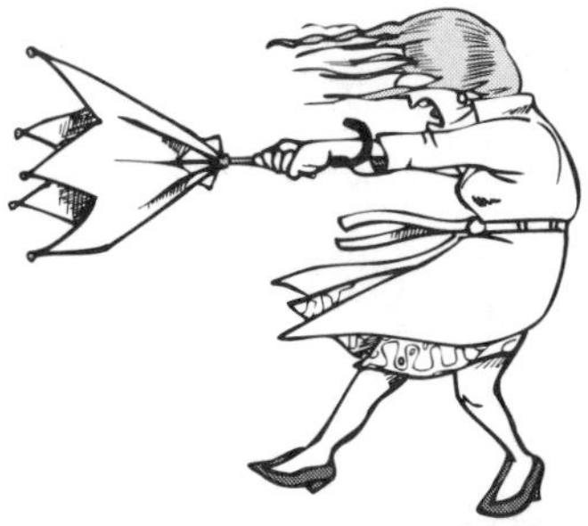

Name: ______________________ **Date:** ______________

Directions: *Read the story below. Then, complete the story map.*

Katie's mom entered her world-famous chili in the State Fair Chili Cook Off. Mrs. Frank spent the entire morning in the kitchen cooking up her family's secret recipe. Katie could smell the aroma from the onions, peppers, ground beef, beans and spices simmering together to make the tasty dish. She grew hungrier by the minute. After hours of preparation, Mrs. Frank called Katie into the kitchen. Katie came running into the kitchen; her mom held out a wooden spoon with her other hand underneath it. "Taste this," asked her mom. As always, the chili was delicious and Katie told her mom she thought it would win first prize.

There were 100 contestants at the State Fair. Katie's mom put her chili pot in front of her number, 29. The judges walked down the rows of chili pots and took a spoonful from each. After each bite, they wrote some comments on a clipboard. Mrs. Frank didn't know what they were writing because judges had to keep everything secret until winners were announced. After 2 hours, they were ready. Katie's mom was nervous. The judges gave Katie's mom's chili pot the red ribbon—second place. Mrs. Frank was so happy. "You'll always be #1 to me," whispered Katie, as she gave her mom a big hug.

Events:

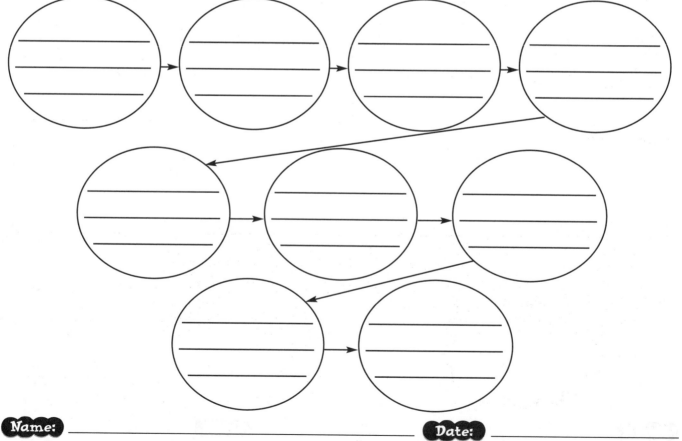

Name: _____   **Date:** _____

Directions: *Read the story below. Then write a sentence explaining each event in the story in the story map below.*

It was a pristine Sunday afternoon. My dad asked me if I would help him with yard work. Since I knew that he loved spending his free time outdoors in the sunshine, I decided to be an agreeable assistant. I love being with my dad so I enjoy our father-son chores.

First, we found all the equipment we would need to mow the lawn and trim the hedges. Next, we checked the gas level inside the lawnmower; it was already full. Finally, my dad put on his favorite baseball cap and a pair of sunglasses. I put on my old hat from summer camp; it was a very sunny day!

Once we got the lawnmower started, my dad showed me how to cut the grass in neat rows. He mowed most of the lawn as I watched. Then he took the trimmer and used it to shape the edges of the lawn. It surely made the lawn look neat. After that, my dad asked me if I was ready to take control of the lawnmower. I mowed the last two rows perfectly! I couldn't believe how easy it was to make my rows just like dad's. When we were all finished, Dad said, "Congratulations on a job well done. I think I'll hand this chore over to you now that you've proved yourself worthy!"

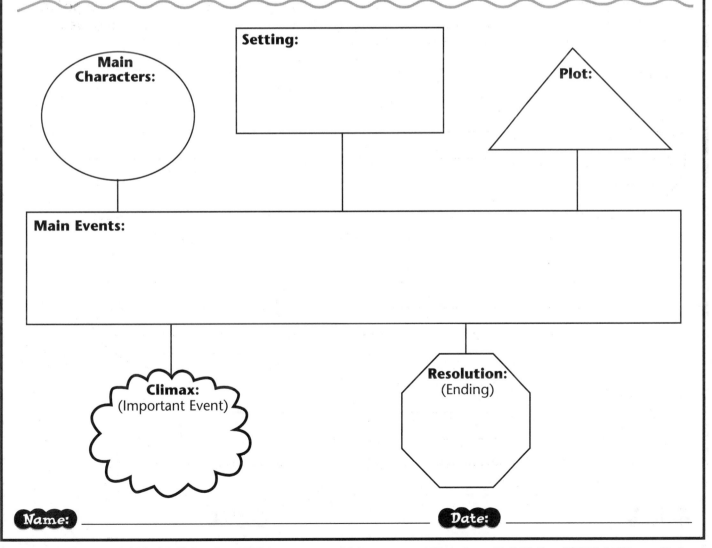

Main Characters:

Setting:

Plot:

Main Events:

Climax:
(Important Event)

Resolution:
(Ending)

Name: _____

Date: _____

I was so excited to go to school on Monday because my mom bought me new sneakers over the weekend. I picked out the navy blue pair of Skippers myself. All the commercials promised that Skippers would make me jump farther and run faster than my old Busters. I couldn't wait to run and play kickball with the kids at school.

On my way to school, I walked faster than usual. I arrived twenty minutes before the bell so some friends and I decided to play chase on the field. I ran so fast that every one commented. I stopped to take a breath, put my hands down on my knees, and when I looked down at my new sneakers—I was in shock. My sneakers were no longer blue but a grimy brown! Even my white shoelaces were stained with mud. Fear struck me like lightning! I just knew I was going to be in big trouble with my mom for being careless. I ran to the boys' bathroom, wet a paper towel, and tried to remove the mud from my new sneakers. It didn't budge. The mud had permanently stained my new shoes!

After school, my mom's van was parked in front of school. I crawled into the van timidly, took a deep breath, and started to tell my mom about my Skippers. I couldn't look her straight in the eye; I felt so awful about my dirty shoes. I hoped she wouldn't be angry with me. To my relief, Mom just smiled, patted my head, and told me that everything was fine. Mom said she bought the sneakers for play. These were my recreation shoes, not my dress shoes. I was so relieved!

Setting _____

Main Characters _____

Plot _____

Events _____

Climax (Important event) _____

Resolution (End) _____

Name: _____   **Date:** _____

My mom and sister are scared of mice. Mice are so small that it's hard for me to fear their presence. Anyway, I'm a boy and boys aren't afraid of furry little creatures. In fact, we like them! My house is near an open field, which makes it convenient for mice to visit our house. When the uninvited guests arrive, it's my job to see that they promptly leave! I make live mousetraps. These traps are fool-proof because they lull the mouse into thinking there is a free cheese meal being served. But when the mouse sits down to eat, SLAM, the trap door closes! No mouse can escape my ingenious trap.

I bait the trap with Swiss cheese, which I have learned is a mouse delicacy. I, too, like putting Swiss cheese on my turkey sandwiches. I use about half a slice for the mousetrap and the other half for myself. I think of these mice as my unwelcome friends. After all, we do have something in common—our love for cheese!

Once I bait the trap and catch a mouse, I usually return it to the field behind our house. I'm convinced the mice tell each other about the food and adventures they have at my house. Why else would so many keep coming back each fall for more cheese?

Narrator:	Problem building up:
What:	
When:	Problem to a head:
The problems: 1. _____ 2. _____	Problem resolved:

Name: _____   Date: _____

For our summer escape, my family and I went on a snorkeling adventure. We live in Hawaii, so you could say the adventure was in our own back yard! First our family drove to the dive store and rented gear: wetsuits, fins, snorkels and goggles. After we tried them on to make sure they fit, we participated in a brief snorkeling training course. We learned how to breathe without using our noses. "Pretend your nose is stuffed and you have a cold," was the instructor's advice. Then the instructor showed us how to properly put on goggles and clean the lenses. When the lesson was finished, we jumped in our Jeep and headed to the beach.

The beach was packed with tourists who had traveled from all over the world to swim with tropical fish and other sea creatures. Luckily for us, no plane fare was necessary! My mom spread out our towels and blankets on the sand and then we put on our gear just as the instructor demonstrated. My dad found a boat that would take us to a secluded lagoon and we all climbed aboard.

Strong waves made the boat ride unpleasant. Finally, we stopped at a lagoon; there were colorful, noisy birds flying overhead. My sister was so excited to see fish swimming so close to our boat. This was her first encounter. We all jumped in the water at once. My family had a great time snorkeling with the fish and exploring the pink coral reefs. After four hours, the boat returned us to the beach where our warm towels and blankets were waiting. We all napped like babies that afternoon!

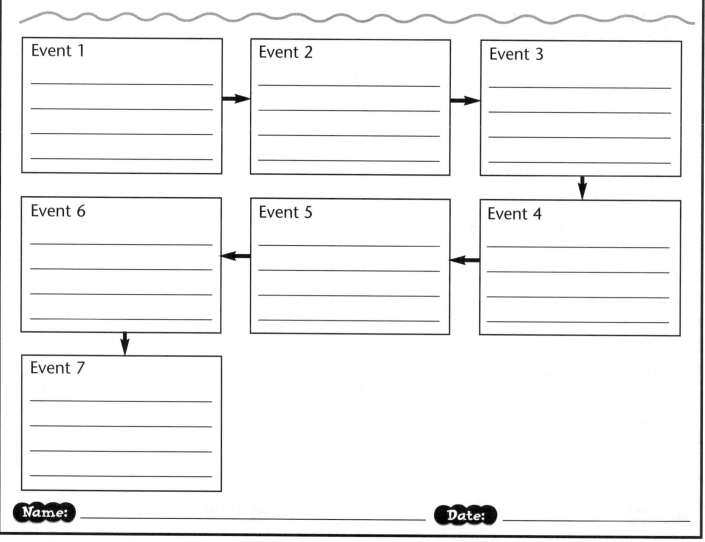

Event 1

Event 2

Event 3

Event 6

Event 5

Event 4

Event 7

Name: _____   Date: _____

On Tuesday, I had a huge end-of-the-year history test. I wanted to prepare for the test properly, so I reread all of my class notes and text assignments. My sister quizzed me on world explorers and dates by turning the questions into a trivia game. On Monday night, I reviewed all of my notes again, and then went to bed early. My mom says it's important to be well rested before a big event.

Mr. Jackson, my history teacher, distributed the test as soon as the commencement bell rang. He walked down each aisle, and placed the tests one by one, upside-down, on each student's desk. I could barely hold my pencil upright; my palms were visibly sweaty.

I wrote my name on the test and then began answering the multiple-choice questions first; they are my favorite. I was on question number 5 when I felt someone peering over my shoulder. I turned to see Ryan looking at my answer sheet. I quickly covered it up with my left hand and continued working. On question 10, I felt Ryan glaring at me. I knew he was livid that I wouldn't let him cheat. But I didn't care. I had studied very hard! How unfair it would be if I gave the answers away to Ryan! Instead of enduring the glare, I picked up my test paper and backpack and walked to an empty desk at the front of the room.

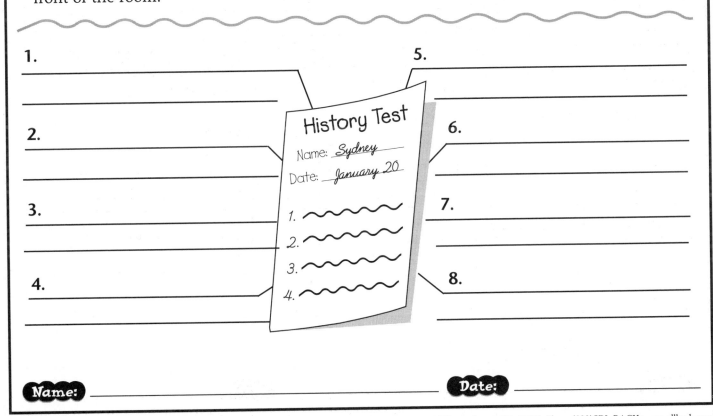

1. _____

2. _____

3. _____

4. _____

5. _____

6. _____

7. _____

8. _____

History Test

Name: *Sydney*

Date: *January 20*

1. ~~~~~~~
2. ~~~~~~~
3. ~~~~~~~
4. ~~~~~~~

Name: _____ **Date:** _____

Jamie and Corey are best friends. One day Jamie told his pal Corey a secret he'd overheard in the office. He softly whispered to Corey that the school was going to host a sundae party for all the fifth graders who had a perfect behavior record. Corey asked Jamie what a perfect behavior record meant. Jamie told him perfect meant a student hadn't been sent to the principal's office or gotten detention the entire year. Corey thought this was a great idea because he was tired of being good without reward—it seemed all the wretched kids were having the most fun.

Corey couldn't take his mind off of the party and kept daydreaming about delicious sundaes with a hot fudge topping and whipped cream. During reading group, Corey leaned over to his group partner, Daniel, and told him the secret. Corey whispered so softly that Daniel misunderstood the secret. Daniel thought that Jamie was having a sundae party and kids had to be on their best behavior to be invited. Daniel was thrilled to be told a secret.

Back at Daniel's desk, his seat partner Matt asked Daniel what he was smiling about. Daniel wasn't a very good secret-keeper. He did not hesitate to tell Matt the great news. "There's going to be a party on Sunday and maybe you can go if Jamie likes you."

Matt wanted to go to the party so badly but he wasn't sure if Jamie knew him. After school, Matt waited for Jamie outside of his classroom. When Jamie exited, Matt asked him, "Can I come to your birthday party on Sunday?"

Jamie looked at Matt curiously, "What are you talking about? I'm not having a birthday party! Where did you hear that? I told Corey the school was having a sundae party!"

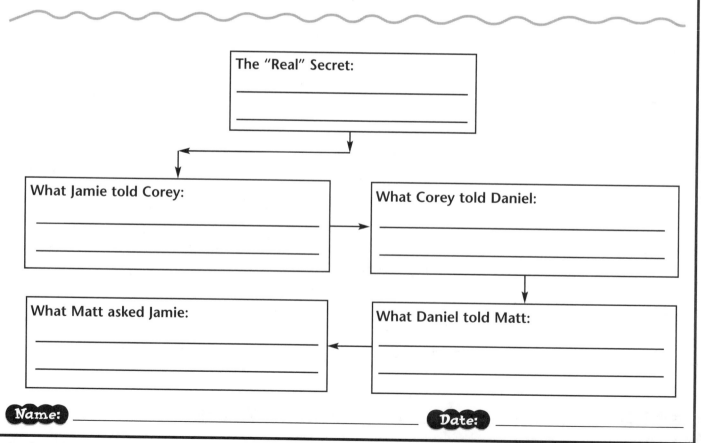

The "Real" Secret:

_____

_____

What Jamie told Corey:

_____

_____

What Corey told Daniel:

_____

_____

What Matt asked Jamie:

_____

_____

What Daniel told Matt:

_____

_____

Scope & Sequence

Students	root words/word origins	prefixes/suffixes	visual/context clues	multiple meaning/signal words	dictionary/glossary	synonyms/antonyms/homonyms	following directions	classification/categorize	analogies	figures of speech	five W's	prediction	main idea	drawing conclusions	context clues	preview/predict outcome	problem/solution	graphic devices	logic matrix	fact/opinion/exaggeration

Scope & Sequence

Students	trivial/redundant information	story order	story genre	topic sentence	compare/contrast	fact/opinion	cause/effect	character analysis	data analysis	inference	reading for detail	story sequence	author's purpose	character's view	plot analysis	character/setting/plot/mood	informative/persuasive writing	factual recall	summarization/generalization	story mapping

Answer Key

Page 6
1. transport
2. dislike
3. inside
4. midnight
5. retake
6. midway
7. uncomfortable
8. disappear
9. misbehave
10. dishonest
Answers will vary.

Page 7
1. pedal
2. centipede
3. pedicure
4. pedestrian
5. pedestal
6. impediment

Page 8
Possible answers:
diagram
dialogue
epigram
epilogue
megalith
megaphone
microgram
microphone
monogram
monograph
monolith
monologue
telegram
telegraph
telephone

Page 9
1. disloyal, loyalty
2. unbeatable, unbeaten
3. undernourished
4. thoughtful, thoughtfulness
5. obsessive, obsession
6. overpaid
7. wondering, wonderful
8. unconditional
9. friendly, friendship
10. adoring, adorable
11. proudly, proudest
12. useless, useable
13. happiness, happiest

Page 10
1. underdone, b
2. mismanaged, a
3. underpaid, a
4. miscalculated, a
5. dislike, b
6. undertone, b
7. dissatisfied, a
8. underweight, b
9. misplaced, a
10. discomfort, b

Page 11
Possible answers.
1. b
2. n
3. l
4. d
5. h
6. a
7. i
8. t
9. m
10. k
11. o
12. e
13. f
14. p
15. g
16. v
17. r
18. j
19. u
20. c
21. q
22. s

Page 12
1. neatest
2. harder, hardest
3. tougher, toughest
4. fastest, faster
5. hardest, harder
6. slower, slowest
7. bravest, braver
8. smallest, smaller
9. older
10. younger, youngest
11. busier, busiest
12. lightest, lighter

Page 13
The following words should be underlined with the suffix circled.
1. approached increasingly worried properly prepared
2. powered combustion
3. barreling
4. maturity loved
5. mighty longest
6. living trailers, combative
7. thoughtful internists, assisted operation
8. originate
9. directive confusion
10. suspicions assumptions troubling situations
11. lightning halted, transmission signals
12. mixture added lightness darkness
13. magical potions
14. invisibility

Page 14
pondered
gift
occasion
wandered
token
bracelet
wallet
policy
earned
redeeming
balance
ornate
anticipation
worthwhile

Page 15
1. a. delicate
2. b. reach
3. b. slight
4. a. distribute
5. a. oral
6. a. instruct
7. a. reject
8. b. catch
9. b. end
10. b. coworkers

Page 16
1. c
2. a
3. a
4. b
5. c
6. b
7. b
8. a
9. a
10. a

Page 17
1. exclaimed, whispered
2. pester, torment
3. inquire, question
4. ancient, prehistoric
5. adequate, sufficient
6. amazed, astonished
7. hazard, peril
8. ripped, tore

Page 18
1. sea turtle
2. whale
3. jellyfish
4. starfish
5. shark
6. crab or lobster
7. seahorse
8. manatee

Page 19
Answers will vary.

Page 20
1. rock

15. moved, forward, backward
2. race
3. trunk
4. darts
5. fence
6. grazed
7. empty
8. legend
9. gorge
10. grave
11. pitcher

Page 21
A. 9 or 21
B. 13 or 23
C. 1 or 17
D. 7 or 11
E. 3 or 22
F. 8 or 16
G. 5 or 18
H. 10 or 27
I. 2 or 20
J. 12 or 26
K. 14 or 25
L. 15, 28
M. 6, 24
N. 4, 19

Page 22
Sequence and Time Signals:
1. when
2. finally
3. lately
4. once
5. immediately
Illustration Signals:
1. such as
2. for example
3. specifically
4. much like
5. similar to
Change of Direction Signals:
1. otherwise
2. rather
3. but
4. however
5. even though

Page 23
Make sure that all five sequence and time signal words are circled in the story.
Initially: when I laid eyes on Smokey, I was more than a bit scared.
Next: I assumed my life was about to go up in flames.
After that: my fear subsided and we became instant friends.
Then: I got a great idea.
Finally: everyone agreed that Smokey was a fine neighbor.

Page 24
Accept reasonable story from Red Riding Hood's point of view. Make sure that all ten signal words are circled in the story:
now
when
suddenly
immediately
much like
when
however
at last
finally
at last

Page 25
1. b	9. a
2. a	10. c
3. b	11. a
4. b	12. b
5. a	13. c
6. a	14. b
7. b	15. a
8. b	

Page 26
1. 2
2. 2
3. han-dle
4. frik-shuhn
5. han-duhl
6. second
7. 3
8. 3
a. 1, b. 3, c.1, d. 2, e. 3, f. 1

Page 27
Ancient: A time long ago
Corpse: A dead body
Curse: An evil spell intended to harm someone.
Embalm: To treat a dead body to protect it from decay.
Legend: A story handed down from earlier times.
Pharaoh: The title of kings of ancient Egypt.
Revenge: Action taken to pay someone back for harm done.
Tomb: A grave, room or building for holding a dead body.
Wrath: Great rage

Page 28
1. trounced
2. declared
3. sprinted
4. enormous
5. cease
6. tiny
7. pleasant
8. fine
9. grave
10. impolite

Page 29
1. terrible
2. never
3. secure
4. shorten
5. enemies
6. fantasy
7. supported
8. brave
9. discontinue
10. stupid
11. tame
12. marvelous

Page 30
1. too, two, to
2. whether, weather
3. sale, sail
4. time, thyme
5. pale, pail
6. male, mail
7. they're, their, there
8. flu, flew, flue

Page 31
a. 10
b. 7
c. 6
d. 5
e. 16
f. 1
g. 2
h. 3
i. 8
j. 13
k. 17
l. 12
m. 9
n. 4
o. 11
p. 14
q. 18
r. 15

Page 32
1. Emerald to Elm
2. Jefferson Parkway
3. south
4. Oak Avenue, east and west
5. Jefferson and Bush
6. east and west
7. The Lake
8. Library
9. The Zoo
10. City Hall

Page 33
a. 9 dozen
b. Add eggs and vanilla
c. Blend in seeds
d. sunflower seeds
e. Answers will vary.
f. granulated and brown sugar
g. Answers will vary.
h. Bake the cookies.
i. Double the recipe.

Page 34
Animals:
Need shelter.
Eat meat and/or plants.
Are able to move.
Plants:
Make their own food.
Turn sunlight into energy.
Have roots.
Both:
Can be eaten by humans.
Need water to survive.
Reproduce
Need air to survive.
Grow
Eliminate waste from their bodies.

Page 35
Fruit
cantaloupe
watermelon
dates
strawberries
grapes
tomatoes
bananas
nectarines
peaches
apples
Vegetables
asparagus
beans
potatoes
radicchio
peppers
Herbs
thyme
chives
basil

Page 36
1. difficult
2. water
3. angry
4. ingredient
5. stop
6. pound
7. king
8. bread
9. wall
10. symphony
11. rough
12. hive
13. referee
14. nine

Page 37
Accept reasonable answer.

Page 38
Answers will vary.

Page 39
a large man; as big as a house
a very fast runner; as quick as a bunny
you had to work to earn money; money doesn't grow on trees
not feeling well; under the weather
ancient; as old as the hills
cease; stop on a dime
cunning; as sly as a fox

Page 40
Itemized store items from the illustration.

Page 41
Accept reasonable answers, which may include the following facts.
Important Facts:
Mrs. Hooper's dog was missing at midnight.
The dog was last seen at 11:47.
Mrs. Hooper heard a loud sawing noise.
Dogs have sensitive ears.
Mrs. Hooper snores.
Unimportant Facts:
The call came on a purple, pocket cell phone.
He always leaves the cell phone on the nightstand.
He put a gray trench coat over his pajamas.
He arrived at Mrs. Hooper's house in 1.4 minutes.
Mrs. Hooper was terrified and panicked.

Page 42
Accept reasonable answers.

Page 43
Malibu
ocean
street clothes
school starts 8:25
walks home
snack recess
sunshine
Chicago
lake
uniforms
school starts 7:55
takes bus
no a.m. recess
windy, rain, and snow
tetherball
Both
body of water nearby
recess
friendship bracelets

Page 44
Questions will vary.

Page 45
Accept reasonable answers.

Page 46
massive butterflies in his stomach; was very nervous

followed in hot pursuit; ran after quickly

stepped on the gas; accelerated quickly

running off at the mouth; excessive talking

cat got your tongue; at a loss for words

whip you into shape; physically challenge

busting at the seams; anxious

let nature run its course; let things go naturally

chasing himself in circles like a rabid dog; panicking

real stinker; tough game

Page 47
1. busy as a bee
2. killed two birds with one stone
3. don't let the bedbugs bite
4. bull by the horns
5. the straw that broke the camel's back
6. something the cat dragged in
7. tongue-tied
8. let the cat out of the bag
9. barn burner
10. under the weather

Page 48
Make sure the story has a headline and contains the information provided for who, what, where, when, and why.

Page 49
1. Virgo
2. June
3. June 22
4. Areas related to publishing, the Internet, telecommunications, computers and software.
5. You will see your name in big letters and lights.

Page 50
Accept reasonable answers.

Page 51
Accept reasonable answers.

Page 52
Accept reasonable answers.

Page 53
Accept reasonable answers.

Page 54
1. chapter 5
2. chapter 4
3. chapter 8

4. chapter 2
5. chapter 2
6. chapter 3
7. chapter 1
8. chapter 6
9. glossary
10. specific page numbers for listings in the book

Page 55
1. Accept another reasonable title for the article.
2. Leonard Estrada
3. Protective suits, gloves and goggles must be worn at all times. Only scientists with Level 5 security clearance are permitted to view the plant. It is being housed at an undisclosed military facility until further testing can be completed.
4. Eyes
5. Accept reasonable answer.
6. To see things in the mind that are not really there.
7. To take in.
8. Answers will vary.
9. Accept reasonable answer.
10. Answers will vary.

Page 56
Accept reasonable answers.

Page 57
Make sure the provided vocabulary words are used in the student story.

Page 58
1. Sunburn definition and prevention.
2. Accept reasonable answers.
3. Swimming safety rules.
4. Accept reasonable answers.

Page 59
1. Joe flies Bob's kite.
2. Accept reasonable answer.
3. Eloise fights for animal rights.

Page 60
Check for one underlined sentence, in each paragraph, that supports the main idea.
1. a
2. b
3. c

Page 61
Accept reasonable answers.

Page 62
1. d
2. a
3. g
4. h
5. i
6. j
7. f
8. e
9. b
10. c

Page 63
1. enemies
2. permission
3. order
4. disappear
5. monument
6. a place in which devotion is paid
7. moved
8. donations
9. a group of people
10. distribution
11. brave and daring

Page 64
1. made up of
2. continue and keep
3. eat
4. made from milk
5. a decrease in bone mass
6. deteriorating
7. older
8. healthy
9. take part in
10. movement activity
11. weight training activity
12. bending of joints

Page 65
Answers will vary.

Page 66
A. 3
B. 5

Page 67
Accept reasonable answers.

Page 68
Accept reasonable answers.

Page 69
1. 25 subscriptions
2. Room 10
3. Room 6
4. Room 14 and Room 18
5. Room 22
6. 11
7. 206
8. Room 4

Page 70
1. 2 servings
2. 100 mg
3. 0 grams
4. Each can contains 2 servings.
5. 1 gram

6. 2 grams
7. 0 mg
8. 230 calories
9. 19 grams
10. dairy group

Page 71
1. The egg is laid.
2. An embryo is formed.
3. The cell splits
4. It's a tadpole.
5. The tadpole changes.
6. Not yet a frog.
7. It's a frog.

Page 72
1. tigers
2. lions and tigers
3. lions
4. tigers
5. lions and tigers
6. lions
7. lions
8. tigers
9. lions and tigers
10. tigers

Page 73
1. Emit Crumm
2. Dopey Dog
3. Lop and Larry
4. Scruffy
5. Dopey Dog and Burt Bunny
6. Scruffy's sidekick
7. Burt Bunny
8. Lop and Larry
9. Emit Crumm
10. Dopey Dog

Page 74
1. England
2. China
3. Australia
4. 50
5. Spain
6. Australia
7. Spain
8. China
9. England
10. 1776

Page 75
1. fact
2. fact
3. fact
4. opinion
5. opinion
6. fact
7. opinion
8. fact
9. opinion
10. fact
11. opinion
12. fact
13. fact
14. fact
15. opinion

16. fact
17. fact
18. opinion
19. opinion
20. fact

Page 76

Joe is ancient—I'd guess about 300 years old.
When Joe was born, the Revolutionary War was just beginning and a kid's idea of fun was chasing squirrels and eating tree bark.
Joe reads 50 books a day and I'm not talking little books, either.
I mean huge tomes, even longer than the telephone directory!
These people had so much stuff in their garage that a worm couldn't even fit in to look around.
And the place smelled like dusty socks were kept there for 100 years.
I thought my nose hairs were going to disintegrate.
Joe must have gotten 1,000 books in his bag!
The darn thing was heavier than an elephant in armor.
I carried them over the mountains and through the woods back to Joe's house.

Page 77

Factual:
Rudd Flynn is thirteen years old.
Electrical storms can be quite dangerous.
He listed safety tips on the warning signs.
Fantasy:
Rudd lives in Trundle.
He is a junior-apprentice sorcerer.
He can cast spells
Rudd produced lightening with a wand.
He magically hung the warning signs.
Gerbilgoff are fanciful creations

Page 78

Rewrite of story without trivial information.

Page 79

Make sure that the story does not include any trivial or redundant information.

Page 80

Make sure that all of the provided sentences have been used to sequence the story. There can be some variation in order.

Page 81

Make sure that all of the provided sentences have been used to sequence the story. There can be variation in order.

Page 82

1. Mystery/Suspense
2. Science Fiction
3. Travel
4. Autobiography

Page 83

7. Biography
8. Self- Help
9. Fiction
10. Non- Fiction

Page 84

A. Nocturnal animals are very different than most animals you commonly see during your waking hours.
B. Nocturnal animals have special adaptations to help them thrive in the dark.
C. Diurnal animals are the opposite of nocturnal animals.

Page 85

Check to see that the following topic sentences are underlined.
The common green iguana, scientifically known as Iguana iguana, is a reptile pet imported from South or Central America and raised in captivity.
Each reptile has requirements for moisture, temperature, hibernation and diet.
Iguanas are diurnal.
Iguanas are a prey species.

Page 86

A. Topic Sentence: Kites have been around for over two thousand years and have had many uses besides recreation.
Supporting Sentences: Kites are believed to have been invented in China or Korea about 200 BC. One of these earliest kite stories is about a famous Chinese general, Han Hsin. Han ordered his men to build a kite and to fly it over the Emperor's palace.
B. Topic Sentence: Rainforests are an important habitat.
Supporting Sentences: Rainforests are home to more than half of those species. Millions of forest-dwelling people around the world live in or depend on rainforests. Many of the world's important food crops, medicines and animals come from rainforest species.
C. Topic Sentence: Boxing Day is a holiday celebrated in Britain, Australia, New Zealand and Canada.
Supporting Sentences: It falls on December 26. The public observance of Boxing Day takes place on the following Monday if December 26 falls on a Saturday or Sunday. The traditional celebration of Boxing Day included giving money and other gifts to charitable institutions, needy individuals and people in service jobs.

Page 87

Topic Sentence: St. Augustine is the oldest permanent European settlement on the North American continent.
Supporting Sentences: It was founded forty-two years before the English colony at Jamestown, Virginia, and fifty-five years before the Pilgrims landed on Plymouth Rock in Massachusetts. Spanish explorer and treasure hunter Don Juan Ponce de Leon first sighted the mainland of the North American on Easter, March 27, 1513. He claimed the land for Spain and named it La Florida, meaning "Land of Flowers".
Topic Sentence: Menendez skillfully fulfilled his king's wishes.
Supporting Sentences: He quickly fortified the tiny village and named it St. Augustine. Making the most of brilliant military maneuvers, Menendez destroyed the French garrison on the St. John's River and, with the help of a tropical hurricane, also defeated the French fleet. With the coast of Florida firmly in Spanish hands, he set to work building the town, establishing missions, converting the Indians to the Church and exploring the lush land.
Check the three fascinating facts.

Page 88

Main Idea: The word carpetbagger was used in the South after the Civil War to describe Northerners who went to the South during reconstruction to seek their fortune.
Supporting Details: Check for reasonable phrases that describe the supporting details.

Page 89

Answers will vary.

Page 90

Similarities: Baseball and golf are both sports.
Both use balls and cleats.
Both can be played on grass or on Astroturf.
Differences: Baseball is a team sport./Golf is an individual sport.
Baseball uses a bat to hit the ball./Golf uses a club to hit the ball.
Different goals.
A lot of running in baseball./ A lot of walking in golf.

Page 91

1. Saturday, October 27 from 8:00-11:00
2. Saturday, October 27 from 12:00-4:00
3. cookies, stew and punch
4. pizza and hot dogs
5. Alice's birthday party
6. Cooper Costume Bash
7. Costume Bash
8. Birthday party
9. Birthday party
10. Answers will vary.

Page 92

Similarities: Both heavily populated cities are the largest in each country. They are major financial and cultural capitals.

Differences: London was once the most influential city in the world, now New York City has taken the lead. New York City is located in the United States and London is the capital of the United Kingdom.

Page 93
1. Both heard a strange noise on October 5th at 11:20.
2. They blamed each other for the flying sand.
3. Accept reasonable answer.

Page 94
1. F	9. O
2. F	10. F
3. F	11. O
4. O	12. O
5. O	13. F
6. F	14. F
7. F	15. O
8. O	

Page 95
1. F
2. F
3. F
4. O
5. F
6. F
7. F
8. O
9. O
10. O
11. F
12. F
13. O
14. F
15. F

Page 96
Cause: Laura overslept in the morning and missed the diving competition.
Effect: Midland did not win a trophy.
Cause: The kids teased Andre so much he decided to walk home alone the long way.
Effect: He rescued a cat and was a hero at school on Monday morning.

Page 97
Accept reasonable answers.

Page 98
Answers will vary.

Page 99
Accept reasonable answers.

Page 100
1. Mattie
2. Azul
3. Victor
4. Jenny
5. 8 students
6. Chris
7. 3:24.48
8. 16.32 seconds
9. Accept reasonable answer.
10. Kerri, James, Sammy, Jenny, Marco, Victor, Olive, Chris.

Page 101
1. Charlie
2. Norman
3. Sharon and Naomi
4. Charlie, because he reads chapter books for 8 hours every week
5. Norman, because he reads cereal boxes for 30 minutes every week.
6. Accept reasonable answer.
7. Answers will vary.
8. Answers will vary.

Page 102
Accept reasonable answers.

Page 103
1. Abe Buffet. Satisfied, sensation, fabulous
2. Water-Detection Wand, because the owner cannot find water.
3. 61 claps
4. Cactus plants hold water.
5. Accept reasonable answers.
Check for a reasonable response to each consumer.

Page 104
1. no	9. no
2. yes	10. yes
3. yes	11. no
4. no	12. no
5. yes	13. no
6. yes	14. yes
7. no	15. no
8. no	

Page 105
1. a	6. b
2. b	7. c
3. c	8. b
4. a	9. b
5. a	10. c

Page 106
Zap- Bands:
1. mosquitoes
2. wrist or ankle
3. summer
4. invisible, odorless
5. no
FullJug:
1. water container
2. Accept reasonable answer.
3. use
4. tropical rain forest
5. one gallon
Stretch Tape:
1. pliable tape
2. Accept reasonable answer.
3. $79.90
4. not many were made
5. first order

Page 107
Accept reasonable answers.

Page 108
a. 9
b. 5
c. 8
d. 7
e. 1
f. 10
g. 4
h. 6
i. 3
j. 2

Page 109
a. 2
b. 5
c. 6
d. 9
e. 7
f. 4
g. 1
h. 3
i. 8
j. 10

Page 110
1. She is happy her grandmother is coming.
2. She thinks her grandmother is very creative.
3. creative, fun, beautiful, thoughtful
4. remarkable, creative, amazing, imaginative
5. A girl who likes her family.
6. Answers will vary.

Page 111
Accept any reasonable answer.

Page 112
Answers will vary

Page 113
A. 1. Mandy does not like sharks, because she fears them.
2. worst animals, dangerous, menaces
B 1. Fletcher thinks sharks are interest beautiful creatures.
2. humble, amazing, beautiful
C. 1. Eva is not too sure about sharks. She's a bit fearful.
2. evil, harmless, hate, protect

Page 114
1. 1940
2. 14 years old
3. her diary
4. She's heard talk of Hitler's armies and extermination of the Jewish people.
5. Her parents tell her the world is too civilized to for Hitler to wipe out an entire population. They are trying to calm her fears.
6. a yellow armband with the Star of David.
7. Her friends are shunning her.
8. She is beginning to suspect everyone of bad things.
9. She is an only child.
10. Answers will vary.

Page 115
1. An outburst of creative activity in art, music, and literature among black Americans.
2. Renaissance means rebirth.
3. New York City's Harlem and Greenwich Village
4. The migration of African Americans from the south to northern cities.
5. Answers will vary.

Page 116
1. The ant was boasting to the chrysalis about how he could move fast, but the chrysalis upstages the ant when it turns into a butterfly.
2. b.
3. Answers will vary.

Page 117
1. The dying father was teaching his sons a lesson.
2. Wise. He was showing his sons a valuable lesson.
3. The task of breaking the sticks is easier if shared by all instead of one.
4. a.
5. Answer will vary.

Page 118
1. beach
2. jungle
3. grocery store
4. jewelry store

5. cemetery
6. ocean
7. car race track
8. zoo
9. outer space
10. school

Page 119
Accept any reasonable answer.

Page 120
1. Old West
2. March 15, 44 BC
3. Revolutionary War
4. Prehistoric
5. Civil War
6. 1960s
7. 1492
8. 1990s
9. Future
10. Present

Page 121
1. Cinderella
2. Romeo & Juliet
3. ET
4. Snow White
5. Little Mermaid
6. Pinocchio
7. Dr. Dolittle
8. Lion King
9. Robin Hood
10. Tarzan

Page 122
Who: Daniel Webster
What: Orator and politician
Where: New Hampshire
Important Information: Webster was in Congress and in the Senate. He ran for president but lost the nomination.
What I Learned: Answers will vary.

Page 123
Answers will vary.

Page 124
1. suspenseful, serious
2. Adam's mother was frantic and when she found Adam she was mad.
3. Adam was in trouble and his mom was mad.
4. Answers will vary.
5. Answers will vary.
6. happy
7. Carlotta and her grandfather are working together to plant the garden.
8. A happy girl and her grandfather planting the garden.
9. Answers will vary.
10. Answers will vary.

Page 125
Accept any reasonable answer.

Page 126
1. balanced meals and exercise
2. grains, vegetables, fruits, milk-products, meats, fish, poultry, and dry beans
3. Foods high in fats or sugars.
4. Play supervised team sports and wear protective gear.
5. Kids do these sports without the proper safety gear.
6. Answers will vary.
7. Answers will vary.
8. Answers will vary.

Page 127
1. T-Rex lived 65 million years ago.
2. T-Rex bones have been found in Montana.
3. T-Rex could run about 30 miles per hour.
4. When T-Rex lost a tooth, another quickly grew in its place.
5. T-Rex is similar to reptiles because it laid eggs, like reptiles.
6. Answers will vary.

Page 128
1. Dogs are helpful to humans in many ways.
2. Water helps people function.
3. Practice helps people become proficient at something they want to learn.
4. The boys have different tastes in movies. The video store offers many movie options.

Page 129
Answers will vary.

Page 130
1. Katie's mom entered the cookoff.
2. Mrs. Frank cooked all morning.
3. Katie tasted the chili.
4. Mrs. Frank place her chili in front of #29 at the contest.
5. The judges tasted the chili from all the other contestants.

6. The judges wrote their comments on clipboards.
7. The judges tasted Mrs. Frank's chili.
8. Mrs. Frank's chili earned the second place ribbon.
9. Katie told her mom she would always be #1 to her.

Page 131
Main characters: father and child
Setting: outdoors in the yard.
Plot: Father and child work in the yard together.
Main Events: father and child cut the grass. Father edges the lawn with the trimmer.
Climax: The father teaches and gives the child a chance to finish cutting the lawn.
Resolution: The child did such a good job, that the child now can add cutting the lawn to his/her chore list.

Page 132
Setting: home and school
Main Character: child and mom
Plot: The child gets new sneakers and gets them dirty the first day.
Events: the child wears the new sneakers to school. The child plays chase before school and gets them dirty.
Climax: The child realizes the shoes are permanently stained.
Resolution: Mom explains the new sneakers are just for play, so it is alright if they got dirty.

Page 133
Narrator: boy
What: Mice invade the house.
When: in the fall
The problems:
1. Mom and sister do not like mice.
2. Mice come into the house from the field.
Problem Building Up: Mice come into the house each fall and the boy has to find a way to get them out.
Problem Head: Mom and sister are scared of the mice and the boy has to get the mice safely out of the house.

Problem Resolved: The boy makes a live mouse trap with Swiss cheese, then releases the captured mice into the field.

Page 134
1. Rented snorkeling gear.
2. Took a snorkeling training course.
3. Headed to the beach.
4. Mom spread our gear on the beach and we got dressed.
5. We got in the boat.
6. We jumped in the water and snorkeled.
7. The boat returned us to the beach, and we napped in the afternoon.

Page 135
1. Prepare for history test.
2. Reread notes and assignment.
3. My sister quizzed me.
4. Review my notes again.
5. Went to bed early.
6. Began taking the test.
7. Noticed Ryan glancing at my paper.
8. Changed desk and finished my test.

Page 136
The "Real" Secret: The school is rewarding good behavior with a sundae party.
Jamie told Corey about the sundae party for good behavior.
Corey told the secret to Daniel.
Daniel told Matt that Jamie was having a party on Sunday.
Matt asked Jamie if he could come to Jamie's Sunday birthday party.